Jackson Pollock's Afternoon

BY RON BARRETT

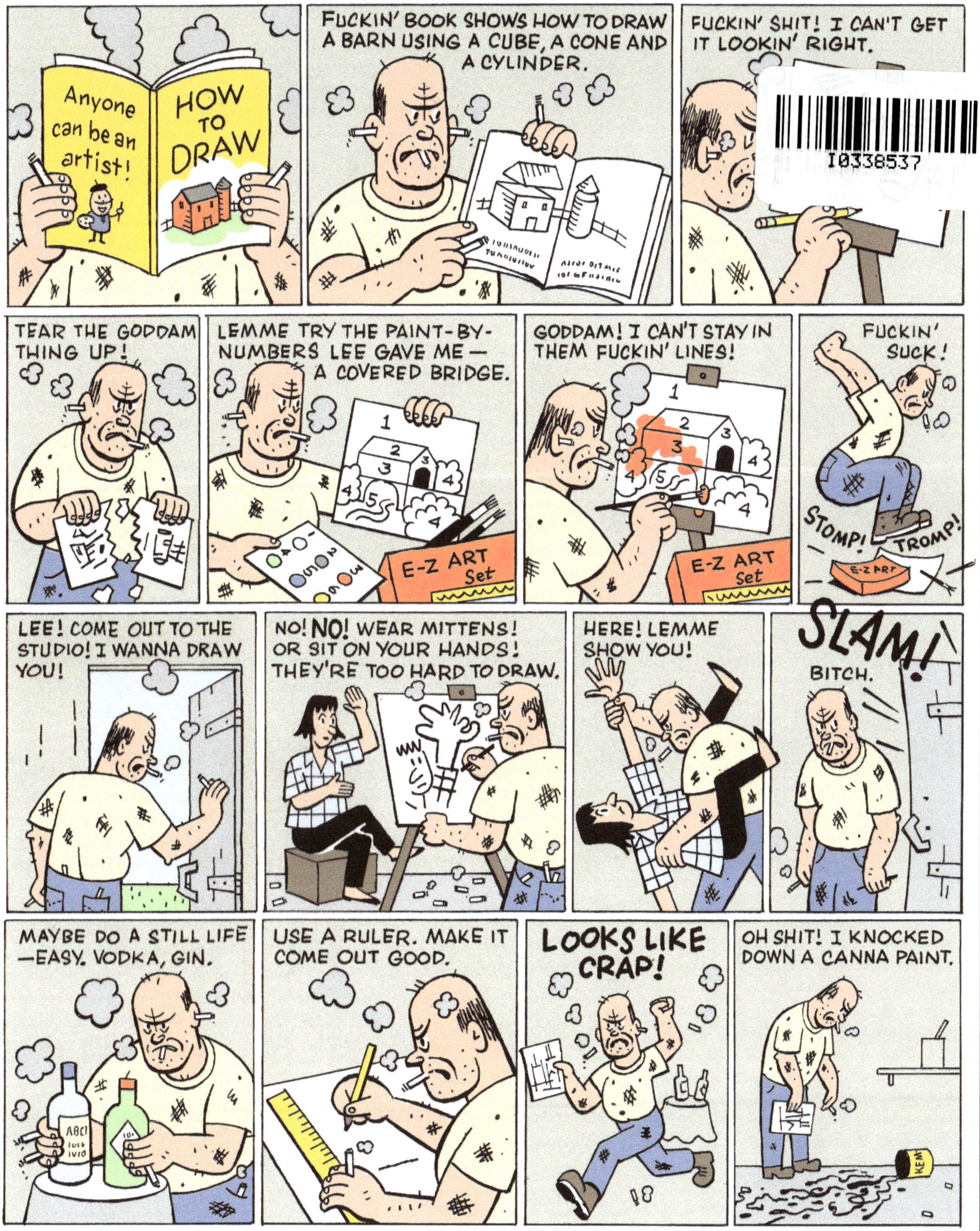
Anyone can be an artist!
HOW TO DRAW
FUCKIN' BOOK SHOWS HOW TO DRAW A BARN USING A CUBE, A CONE AND A CYLINDER.
FUCKIN' SHIT! I CAN'T GET IT LOOKIN' RIGHT.
TEAR THE GODDAM THING UP!
LEMME TRY THE PAINT-BY-NUMBERS LEE GAVE ME — A COVERED BRIDGE.
E-Z ART Set
GODDAM! I CAN'T STAY IN THEM FUCKIN' LINES!
E-Z ART Set
FUCKIN' SUCK!
STOMP!
TROMP!
LEE! COME OUT TO THE STUDIO! I WANNA DRAW YOU!
NO! NO! WEAR MITTENS! OR SIT ON YOUR HANDS! THEY'RE TOO HARD TO DRAW.
HERE! LEMME SHOW YOU!
SLAM!
BITCH.
MAYBE DO A STILL LIFE —EASY. VODKA, GIN.
USE A RULER. MAKE IT COME OUT GOOD.
LOOKS LIKE CRAP!
OH SHIT! I KNOCKED DOWN A CANNA PAINT.

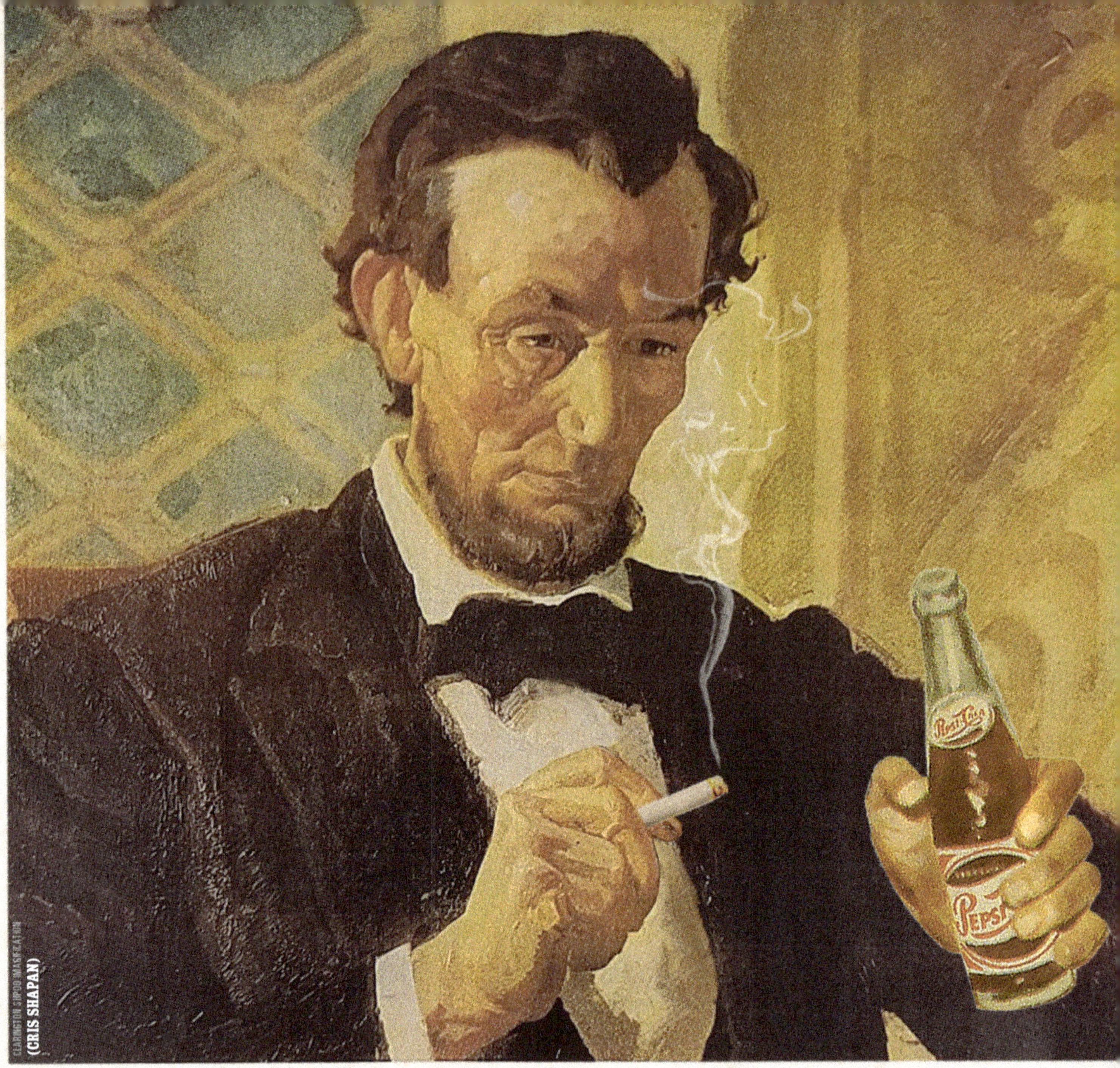

(CRIS SHAPAN)
Pepsi-Cola
Pepsi

All I wanted was a **Pepsi!**

"I was in the "Me" Bedroom, and I was just, like, staring at the wall, thinking about everything...But then again, I was thinking about nothing. And then Secretary of War Stanton came in; I didn't even know he was there. He called my name, and I didn't even hear it. And then he started screaming,
'Mr. President! Mr. President!'
And I go, What, what's the matter?
And he goes, 'What's the matter with you?'
I go, There's nothing wrong, Mr. Secretary.
And he goes, 'Don't tell me that, you're on laudanum!'
I go, No, sir, I'm neither on laudanum nor paragoric, I'm in hale and hardy condition. In fact - I was just thinking, you know - why don't you get me a Pepsi?"

ABRAHAM LINCOLN, *1864*

These words spoken by Abraham "Mike" Lincoln state a principle which we at Pepsi strive to follow in our daily endeavors: Pepsi is here to provide refreshment to *everyone*, regardless of their mental state. Lincoln was under tremendous stress at the time, trying to unite a fractured republic, abolish slavery, and dodge his whack-a-doo wife, who was often lurking behind the furniture.

Would you truly deny him a Pepsi, *just one Pepsi*, just because he doesn't feel like talking? After all, he went to *your* schools, *your* church, *your* House of Representatives. C'mon - don't judge him by his big hat or his sullen demeanor, *just give him refreshment*.

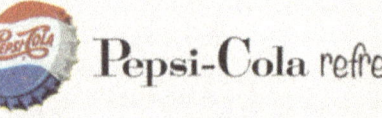

Pepsi-Cola refreshes without judgement

SENIOR EDITOR'S LETTER
BY ALAN GOLDBERG
FOR SURE
The American Bystander: The Lost Years

After Jenny Boylan's wonderful piece on the original 1982 pilot issue of *The American Bystander*, many people have asked, "OK, but why did it take 35 years to come back?

Let me tell you...

It all started at Channel 13, New York's public TV station, where I was a writer and producer. In those golden, low-budget days, WNET was open to just about anything—a live show, for example, where John and Yoko invited audience members to climb a stepladder and jump off. That kind of programming didn't last long, though I understand the lawsuit from the broken leg took a decade to settle.

In 1976, *SNL* writer Brian McConnachie was hired to do short pieces in-between programs which I produced. An Upper East Side version of *Porgy and Bess*, for example, called "Porter and Beth." Or a book chat where both interviewer and interviewee wore S&M masks. (Sample questions: "Is your favorite author Edna St. Louis, Missouri?" "Have you had that experience, too, of being at home reading when your bookshelves just start wandering around the room?")

We became good friends, in no small part because it was such a pleasure to hang out with Brian. His humor is more than original; it presents the world in ways no one could ever have imagined. But common sense is something we both have wrestled with.

For example, out behind Brian's house sat a beautiful but decaying wooden gazebo. I volunteered to help him disassemble it, find some replacement pieces, then put it back together. We took it apart in no time—I'm kinda handy—then realized we hadn't made a single note on how all these many, many pieces fit together. We laughed, Brian's wife Ann not as much.

ALAN GOLDBERG is Senior Editor of *The American Bystander*.

The next day, Brian tried to explain what happened to his daughter, Mary: "A strong wind blew it over."

"No daddy, she said, "It fainted."

In the 1980s, I continued my life as a writer and producer of non-fiction TV—a history of epidemic diseases was typical; none were remotely funny. Brian, on the other hand, had soothed his post-*Bystander* disappointment by gathering *Lampoon Radio Hour* friends to tape bits of humor: "Tales of the UN Peacekeep-

GAZEBO-KILLERS: *Alan, Brian & Mary in 1988.*

ers," "Dave Gilmore, Nude Accountant," and "Tina Destiny, Space Commander."

By the mid-90s, these get-togethers had coalesced into a wonderful shaggy dog serial of Brian's, *Big Ship Radio*, about a mothballed battle cruiser turned into the world's worst cruise ship. Joined by Emily Prager and Ed Subitsky, the four of us recorded the first two scripts at a midtown studio. We knew we had the next great public radio show.

And then—a lost twenty years.

Neither Brian nor I knew exactly how to fund a radio show, or how to get public stations to air it. But we are both friendly, somewhat gullible guys ready to believe that anyone offering help must know what they're doing. And so began a parade of (mostly) well-meaning folks who, like all of us, were attracted to Brian and his wondrous humor. All the helpers had plausible credentials, so when they asked to help, we said, "Sure."

The first was a man we'll call "Charles Fitts"—nice guy, enthusiastic, many ideas, lost interest. In his honor, the word "Fittsian" was applied to each successive savior, as the months mounted and we realized we'd fallen down yet another rabbit hole. Other Fittsians included a sometime Broadway producer who was sure he could convince his rich wife to fund us, and a British expert in comedy currently coaching a girl's school soccer team. Not one of these forays took less than a year of meetings, ideas, promises, and more meetings—just to get back to where we started.

So how did *The Bystander* come back? I will take full credit for the idea of reviving it. After our fabulous lack of success on *Big Ship Radio*, I called Brian one day in 2002, and said maybe we could revive *The American Bystander*...as a website.

Brian liked the idea but, once again, neither of us had any clue how. Thus began *Big Ship* redux, with a number of very pleasant lunches with very pleasant friends, none of whom who could help.

Around 2007, Brian gave a talk at Yale University, as a guest of *The Yale Record* college humor magazine. This was arranged by Michael Gerber, *Record* alum and lover of print humor magazines. He listened to our schemes with interest.

You have to know this about Michael. He is the least Fittsian person on the face of the earth. He immediately had good ideas, the most important of which was to make the new *Bystander* print. Print?!! Now if Brian and I were not who we are, we might have fought more strenuously against what turned out to be a brilliant idea. Instead, as always, we said, "Sure."

And, for once, it turned out to be exactly the right answer. ⓑ

TABLE OF CONTENTS

The AMERICAN BYSTANDER
#12 • Vol. 3, No. 4 • Aug/Sept 2019

EDITOR & PUBLISHER
Michael Gerber
HEAD WRITER
Brian McConnachie
SENIOR EDITOR
Alan Goldberg
ORACLE Steve Young
STAFF LIAR P.S. Mueller
INTREPID TRAVELER
Mike Reiss
AGENTS OF THE SECOND BYSTANDER INTERNATIONAL
Craig Boreth, Matt Kowalick, Neil Mitchell, Maxwell Ziegler
MANAGING EDITOR EMERITA
Jennifer Boylan
CONTRIBUTORS
Lila Ash, Penny Barr, Ron Barrett, Art Baxter, Barry Blitt, Roy Blount, Jr,., George Booth, Emma Brewer, Mark Bryan, Roz Chast, Tom Chitty, Seymour Chwast, Cassidy Cummings, John Cuneo, Joe Dator, Scott Dikkers, Nick Downes, Ben Doyle, Marques Duggans, Bob Eckstein, David Etkin, Xeth Feinberg, Emily Flake, Mort Gerberg, Sam Gross, Lance Hansen, Ron Hauge, Greg Hess, Sarah Hutto, John Jonik, Ted Jouflas, Frley Katz, Patrick Kennedy, Lars Kenseth, Jennifer Kim, Paul Kleba, Adam Koford, Riane Konc, Paul Krassner, Sean LaFleur, Paul Lander, Sara Lautman, Stan Mack, Ann McConnachie, Ross MacDonald, Walt Maguire, Sandra Moore, Tom Motley, Jeremy Nguyen, David Ostow, Oliver Ottisch, Jonathan Plotkin, K.A. Polzin, Matt Powers, Simon Rich, Laurie Rosenwald, Curtis Retherford, Alex Schmidt, Cris Shapan, Edward Sorel, Rich Sparks, Ed Subitzky, Eugenia Viti, D. Watson, Andrew Weldon, Phil Witte, Kristopher Wood, & Jonathan Zeller.
THANKS TO
Kate Powers, Lanky Bareikis, Jon Schwarz, Alleen Schultz, Molly Bernstein, Joe Lopez, Eliot Ivanhoe, Neil Gumenick, Kate Ingold, Greg & Patricia Gerber and many others.
NAMEPLATES BY
Mark Simonson
ISSUE CREATED BY
Michael Gerber

Vol. 3, No. 4. ©2019 Good Cheer LLC, all rights reserved. Proudly produced in good ol' California, USA.

ROSS MACDONALD

DEPARTMENTS
Frontispiece: "Jackson Pollock's Afternoon" **by Ron Barrett** . 1
"I Just Wanted a Pepsi **by Cris Shapan** 2
Senior Editor's Letter **by Alan Goldberg** 3
The Good Stuff: Art, Part 1 8
"Mr. Nice Guy" **by Ed Sorel** 76

GALLIMAUFRY
Ron Hauge, Oliver Ottisch, Walt Maguire, Alex Schmidt, David Etkin, Eugenia Viti, Ben Doyle, Sandra Moore, Curtis Retherford, Paul Lander, Sarah Hutto, Tom Chitty, Cassidy Cummings, Patrick Kennedy, Art Baxter, Matt Powers, Rich Sparks, Lars Kenseth, Phil Witte, Greg Hess, Lila Ash, Kristopher Wood.

SHORT STUFF
Meal Life **by Roz Chast** 5
My Comic-Con Hotel Room **by John Cuneo** 7
Unindicted Co-Conspirators
  by Paul Krassner and Mort Gerberg 12
I Was Wrong: The Zombie Apocalypse
  Will Kill Humans Before Climate Change **by Al Gore** 25
Ten Incredibly Short People You Didn't Know
  Were Celebrities **by Roy Blount, Jr.** 26
I Am An Artist **by Jennifer Kim** 28
Can I Be Real With You For a Second? **by Yankee Doodle** ... 30

MEAL LIFE

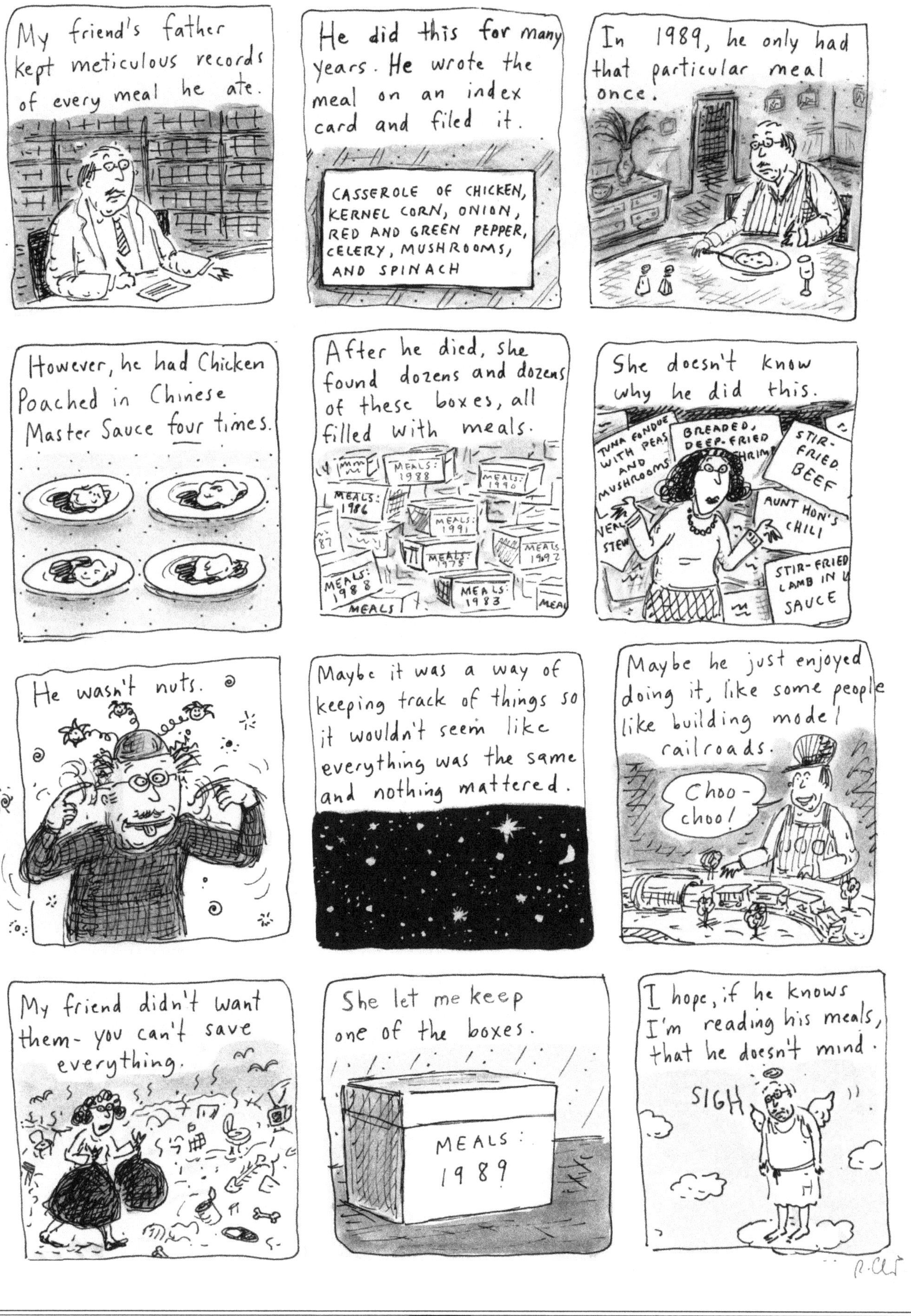
My friend's father kept meticulous records of every meal he ate.
He did this for many years. He wrote the meal on an index card and filed it.
CASSEROLE OF CHICKEN, KERNEL CORN, ONION, RED AND GREEN PEPPER, CELERY, MUSHROOMS, AND SPINACH
In 1989, he only had that particular meal once.
However, he had Chicken Poached in Chinese Master Sauce four times.
After he died, she found dozens and dozens of these boxes, all filled with meals.
MEALS: 1988
MEALS: 1990
MEALS: 1986
MEALS: 1991
MEALS: 1975
MEALS: 1992
MEALS: 1988
MEALS: 1983
MEALS
She doesn't know why he did this.
TUNA FONDUE WITH PEAS AND MUSHROOMS
BREADED, DEEP-FRIED
STIR-FRIED BEEF
AUNT HON'S CHILI
STEW
STIR-FRIED LAMB IN
SAUCE
He wasn't nuts.
Maybe it was a way of keeping track of things so it wouldn't seem like everything was the same and nothing mattered.
Maybe he just enjoyed doing it, like some people like building model railroads.
Choo-choo!
My friend didn't want them - you can't save everything.
She let me keep one of the boxes.
MEALS: 1989
I hope, if he knows I'm reading his meals, that he doesn't mind.
SIGH

Three Secret DJ Tips For the "Twilight of the West"
 by DJ Dirty Needle..32
Wanted: High-Conflict, Paranoid Baby Boomer
 to Run Essential Department *by Emma Brewer*.............34

SPECIAL SECTION: "INKY FINGERS"
The Big Idea *by Jonathan Plotkin*................................37
My Comedy Albums *by Joe Dator*................................28
Cartoons *by Jeremy Nguyen*..40
Birds on the Wing *by D. Watson*..................................41
Cartoons *by Andrew Weldon*.......................................42
To the Rescue… *by J. Jonik*..43
One Day In The Park *by Ed Subitzky*..........................44
Emergency Care For The Choking Victim *by Tom Motley*....45
Phantasy Phashions *by Seymour Chwast*....................46
Welcome to the Shit-Show *by Mark Bryan*.................48
Cartoons *by Paul Kleba*..50
An Interview with Marty Gross *by Lance Hansen*........51
Small Failures *by Xeth Feinberg*...................................56
Next! *by Adam Koford*..57
Architecture Journal *by Sara Lautman*........................58
My Moscowitz *by Stan Mack*.......................................60
Cartoons *by David Ostow*..61
The Red Menace *by Sam Gross*..................................62
Cartoonists in Cars Getting Agita
 by Bob Eckstein & Nick Downes................................64
Is A Floating Home For You? *by Penny Barr*...............65
The Wasps *by Ted Jouflas*..66

OUR BACK PAGES
P.S. Mueller Thinks Like This *by P.S. Mueller*..............69
Time-Travel Study Buddies *by Simon Rich & Farley Katz*..71
What Am I Doing Here? *by Mike Reiss*.......................73

CARTOONS & ILLUSTRATIONS BY
C. Shapan, R. MacDonald, J. Cuneo, M. Gerberg, R. Hauge, O. Ottisch, E. Viti, S. Moore, T. Chitty, A. Baxter, R. Sparks, P. Witte, L. Ash, B. Blitt, L. Rosenwald, L. Hansen, E. Flake, M. Duggans, D. Reiss.

"When the light starts to dim, insert two fresh AA batteries up his ass."

COVER

I liked **Joe Ciardiello** from the first moment we met, tucked away at a table in the third-floor bar of the Society of Illustrators one cold night in February 2018. It was loud and I had to crane in close to hear, and even though the air was heavy with my signature scent—"Sweaty Tweed"—Joe was nice as pie. The International Order of Beatlefans might kick me out for running this cover, but it's just too wonderful a rendition of Mick and the boys to pass up. Thank you, Joe, and next time we're at SOI, the drink's on me.

ACKNOWLEDGMENTS

All material is ©2019 its creators, all rights reserved; please do not reproduce or distribute it without written consent of the creators and *The American Bystander*. The following material has previously appeared, and is reprinted here with permission of the author(s): Mort Gerberg's cartoon on page 11 was originally published in *The Realist* in 1962. And Lance Hansen's Marty Grosz piece appeared in *The Nation*'s OppArt website. Everything else… new, new, new!

THE AMERICAN BYSTANDER, Vol. 3, No. 4, (ISBN TK TK TK). Publishes ~4x/year. ©2019 by Good Cheer LLC. No part of this magazine can be reproduced, in whole or in part, by any means, without the written permission of the Publisher. For this and other queries, email *Publisher@ americanbystander.org*, or write: Michael Gerber, Publisher, *The American Bystander*, 1122 Sixth St., #403, Santa Monica, CA 90403. Subscribe at www.patreon.com/bystander. Other info can be found at www.americanbystander.org.

JOHN CUNEO

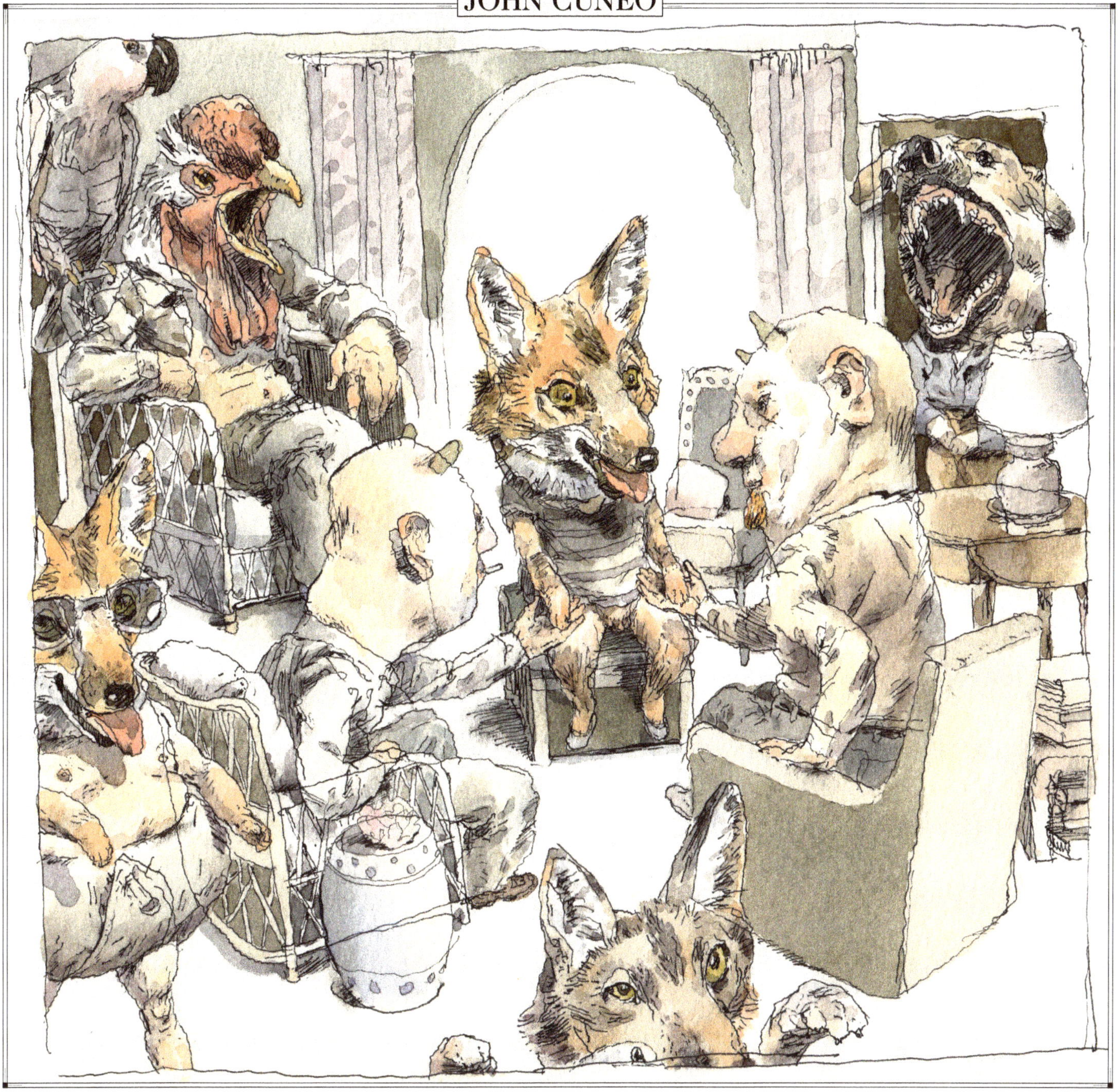

TARGETED ADVERTISING SURVEY

Despite its many advantages, *The American Bystander*'s print-centric model means that we cannot easily gather the vast sums of personal data today's advertisers demand. To give us a boost against our internet-based comedy competition, we are asking *truly dedicated* readers to fill out the following short survey. Your responses will help provide more value to our advertisers and—in a few instances—Federal law enforcement. *Thanks!*

1. Please list the titles of the articles you read in this issue, and how long you spent on each. (HH:MM:SS format)
2. Log where you read this issue (latitude/longitude), with the corresponding times.
3. Did you read the magazine during defecation? Did it seem to have any effect(s)?
4. Shout your Social Security number as loud as you can. We're listening.
5. Please provide samples of hair, blood, and semen/ova for DNA testing.
6. Yes, our advertisers certainly do need your semen/ova. Look, do you want to support quality humor writing or not?
7. What is the one secret you *never* want anyone to know?
8. Did your eyes linger on any photos or illustrations in this issue? If so, which ones and for how long? (HH:MM:SS format)
9. Using your smartphone, please record any conversations you have regarding this issue of *The American Bystander*. Forward these, along with copies of any written correspondence about its contents.
10. Do you agree to our Privacy Policy? I mean, *really* agree to it? The Policy is easily accessible in a 6,000-page document etched into vanadium tablets buried deep within an asphalt-lined vault located a mile beneath *Bystander* headquarters here in Santa Monica, CA. We can't go into all the stuff that's in there, because it's pretty complicated, but we're assuming you're fully on board. If you don't agree, please send a certified letter, signed by your lawyer and witnessed by a notary, stating simply "NO!" (Font of your choice, but 144-point or above, please.)
11. Are you thinking about your ex?
12. If "yes," explain, keeping in mind that our advertisers are notorious perverts (see #6).
13. Consider: do you really even know yourself? If not, how can our advertisers ever expect to know you? Take some time to meditate, and then reflect in 500 words or so on what you've learned about yourself, and how those insights might help *The American Bystander* and its multifarious corporate partners sell you some crap.

—Jonathan Zeller

READER SERVICE

THE GOOD STUFF: ART, PART 1
Adjust your library accordingly

Turns out the answer to the question, "How long will it take for us to start repeating ourselves?" is precisely eight issues. But we're all friends here, and as I cast a bleary eye over our first annual "Inky Fingers" issue—a light Bystander tilted towards art, cartooning and illustration—I felt it needed a little heft, a touch of history, a dash of perspective. Then I remembered Bystander #4, where I asked our contributors for their must-have comedy movies, books and TV, and called the resulting list "The Good Stuff." This time the question was a little tougher: "Which art/illustration/cartooning books are must-own? Which helped make you the person you are today?" Our contributors, as you might imagine, fairly boiled over with suggestions...so this is merely the first half; the sequel will be in the next issue.

Abstract City by Christophe Niemann *(Andrew Weldon)*
Addams and Evil by Charles Addams *(Larry Doyle) (John Jonik)*
Advanced Cartooning by B. Kliban *(Adam Koford)*
The Adventures of Phoebe Zeit-Geist by Michael O'Donahue and Frank Springer *(Larry Doyle)*
Aesthetics by Ivan Brunetti *(Lance Hansen)*
Al Jaffee's Mad Life by Mary-Lou Weisman *(Jeff Kulik)*
All in Line by Saul Steinberg *(Tracey Berglund)*
America by Ralph Steadman *(Ron Hauge)*
Amphigorey by Edward Gorey *(Nick Spooner) (Andrew Weldon)*
Amphigorey Too by Edward Gorey *(Nick Spooner)*
...And Then We'll Get Him by Gahan Wilson *(Shannon Wheeler)*
The Apex Treasury of Underground Comics *(Sam Henderson)*
The Art in Cartooning by Edwin Fisher, Mort Gerberg and Ron Wolin *(Mort Gerberg)*
The Art of Harvey Kurtzman: The Mad Genius of Comics by Denis Kitchen and Paul Buhle *(Will Pfeifer)*
The Art of Humorous Illustration by Nick Meglin *(Ian Baker)*
The Art of Jack Davis by Hank Harrison *(Ian Baker)*
The Art of *The New Yorker* 1925-1993 by Lee Lorenz *(Matt Percival)*
The Art of Will Eisner by Cat Yronwode *(Rich Sparks)*
The Art of William Steig *(Tracey Berglund)*
As I See by Boris Artzybasheff *(Sport Murphy)*
At Home with Rick Geary Collected Stories 1977-85 *(David Chelsea)*
Backing into Forward: A Memoir by Jules Feiffer *(Larry Doyle)*
The Basil Wolverton Collection by Basil Wolverton *(Shannon Wheeler)*
The Best of Gluyas Williams *(David Chelsea) (Rick Geary)*
Black and White: Being the Early Illustrations of Maxfield Parrish *(David Chelsea)*
Blitt by Barry Blitt *(Tracey Berglund)*
Bloom County 1986-1989 Classics of Western Literature by Berkeley Breathed *(Matt Percival)*
Book by Modern Toss *(Andrew Weldon)*
The Book of Shrigley by David Shrigley *(Andrew Weldon)*

Can't We Talk About Something More Pleasant? By Roz Chast *(Andrew Weldon)*
Caricature by Dan Clowes *(Lance Hansen) (Will Pfeifer)*
Cartoon County: My Father and His Friends in the Golden Age of Make-Believe by Cullen Murphy *(Patrick Kennedy)*
The Cartoon History Of The Universe by Larry Gonick *(Alex Schmidt)*
Cartooning for Everybody by Lawrence Lariar *(Mort Gerberg)*
Cartooning: Philosophy and Practice by Ivan Brunetti *(Lance Hansen)*
Cartoons Even We Wouldn't Dare Print edited by Sean Kelly *(Kit Lively)*
Cat Getting Out of a Bag and Other Observations by Jeffrey Brown *(Alicia Kraft)*
The Cat Whose Whiskers Slipped by Ruth Campbell, Illustrated by Ve Elizabeth Cadie *(Sport Murphy)*
The Cobb Book by Ron Cobb *(Andrew Weldon)*
The Collected Hairy Who Publications edited by Dan Nadel *(Lance Hansen)*
Comics (1974) by *The National Lampoon* *(Sam Henderson)*
The Complete Crumb, Vols. 1-18, by Robert Crumb *(Shannon Wheeler) (Ken Krimstein) (Ron Hauge) (Joe Oesterle)*
The Complete Dream of the Rarebit Fiend (1904-1913) by Windsor McCay *(David Chelsea)*
The Complete Far Side by Gary Larson *(K.A. Polzin) (Ron Hauge) (Joe Oesterle)*
The Complete Cartoons of *The New Yorker* *(Joe Oesterle)*
The Complete Calvin and Hobbes by Bill Watterson *(Riane Konc) (Joe Oesterle)*
The Cowboy Wally Show by Kyle Baker *(Larry Doyle) (Shannon Wheeler)*
The Dark Knight by Frank Miller *(Shannon Wheeler)*
Degenerate Art: The Exhibition Catalogue Guide *(Lance Hansen)*
Different Dances by Shel Silverstein *(Larry Doyle)*
Down the Street by Lynda Barry *(K.A. Polzin)*
Drawing Words and Writing Pictures by Jessica Abel and Matt Madden *(Geoffrey Golden)*
Drawn and Quartered by Charles Addams *(Larry Doyle)*
Ed, The Happy Clown by Chester Brown *(Andrew Weldon)*
Eddie Deco's Last Caper by Gahan Wilson *(Jim Siergey)*
Eyebeam by Sam Hurt *(Larry Doyle)*

(THE GOOD STUFF continues on page 74)

This advertisement is authorised by ⊙ Scarfolk Council

"Scarfolk might be the most satisfying bit of sustained satire I've encountered since, well, The Onion"
— Dangerous Minds

"Meticulously detailed and impressively creepy"
— Atlas Obscura

"We've never had to deal with a more glaring example"
— Case CR98-1: Contravention of the Psychological Torture Act. New York County Court Files

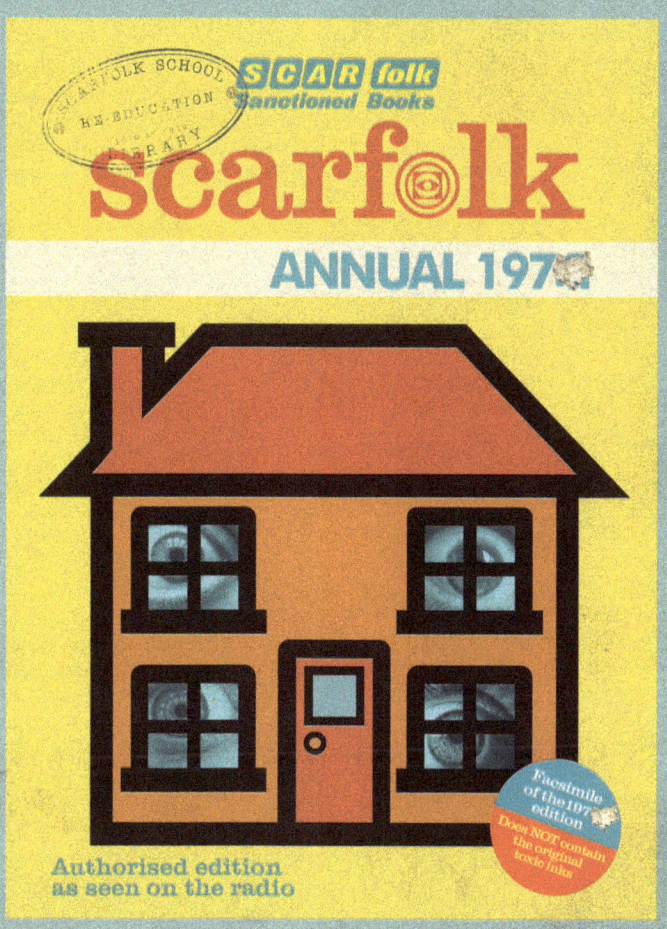

Available from:
Amazon, Barnes & Noble, Indiebound, Books-A-Million & others

For more information please re-read

SPOTLIGHT
BY MORT GERBERG & PAUL KRASSNER
UNINDICTED CO-CONSPIRATORS
The Sunshine Boys have one final schmooze

In June, I asked the cartoonist Mort Gerberg to have a chat with his longtime friend and collaborator Paul Krassner, creator of **The Realist**. Their mission, should they choose to accept it, was to sum up in words and pictures their six-decade friendship and collaboration. They took to the assignment with relish, as I knew they would—Mort and Paul are suckers for the noble effort, the impossible dream. That's why theirs is a friendship worth reading about.

On July 21st, as Mort and I were making a last few changes, Paul died suddenly, giving the conversation below an extra poignancy. There surely wouldn't be a **Bystander** if there hadn't been Paul's **Realist**—and it's impossible to imagine that magazine without the wonderful sparks struck between this pair of friends. So let's raise a glass to Mort, and say hail and farewell to Paul, one of the twentieth century's greatest satirists. —MG

PAUL: I was trying to remember when you and I first met. Was it 1960?
MORT: 1961. I'd just returned to NYC after a year in Mexico, and was starting to freelance. Marvin Kitman told me about *The Realist*. He said it was "irreverent."
PAUL: You were ahead of your time—with your cartoons and that goatee of yours! Very hip, very 60's.
MORT: And you were very clever. At lunch, I tapped a glass of water and you declared, "F-sharp!" You had perfect pitch in music as well as words.
PAUL: You could really draw well, and I liked your ideas that spun off timely subjects.

MORT: But your ideas were about what *might* happen—outrageous. And you had that guileless baby face.
PAUL: Well, never judge a kook by his cover.
MORT: Remember that party in the Village?
PAUL: The host looked at your goatee and at me, and immediately assumed that Mort was Paul...
MORT: ...and Paul was Mort.
PAUL: We switched identities for the rest of the evening. Nobody had a clue.
MORT: We had a lot of unexpected reality twists.
PAUL: Like that cartoon of yours I published: The Old Woman in a Shoe asks a Dr. Burnhill if he "could perform a certain operation"...
MORT: ...and you phoned me late at night, to ask how I made up the abortionist's name. I was in Brooklyn living with my parents, so I whispered, "I just made it up, why do you ask?"

From **The Realist** *#35, June 1962.*

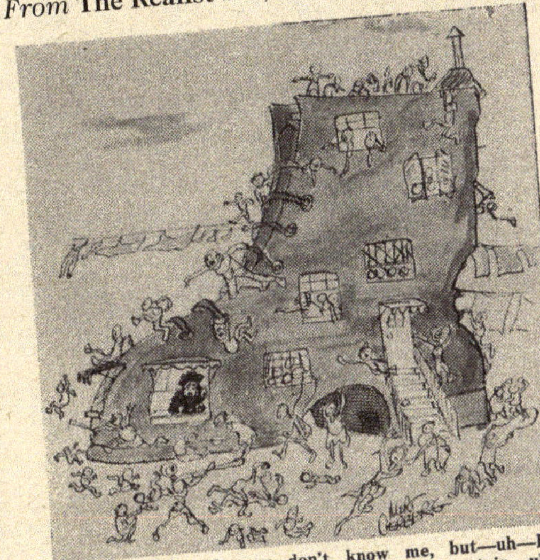

"Dr. Burnhill?—uh—you don't know me, but—uh—I've been told that you could—uh—perform a certain—uh—operation—"

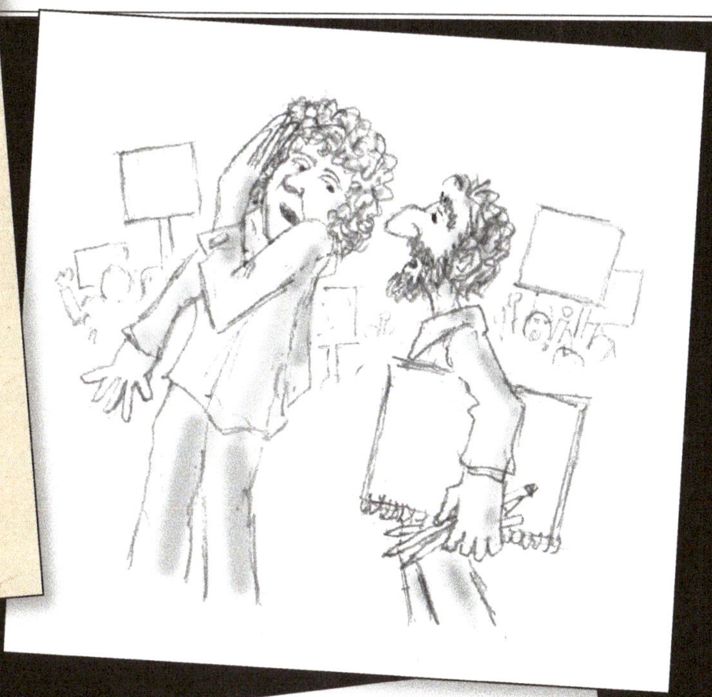

PAUL: So I told you there was a real Dr. Burnhill—-from Brooklyn....who called me in distress after patients started bringing him that issue of *The Realist*. You were afraid he'd sue. I apologized to him.

In his "honor," almost every subsequent *Realist* cartoon of yours had a character named Burnhill.

MORT: How about when I was sketching at the '68 Democratic Convention, and I spotted you at a protest in Lincoln Park and rushed over to say hello...

PAUL: ...But I whispered, "Pretend you don't know me, I'm being followed by the FBI."

MORT: I thought you were kidding; you were talking out of the side of your mouth like Humphrey Bogart.

PAUL: But I really *was* being followed by the FBI—for days—so the joke was on you!

MORT: You would always say: "It's impossible to make this stuff up."

PAUL: It's even harder now. The people today are even more unbelievable. Reality TV shows are playing in real life.

MORT: So, Paul, what can old satirists do?

PAUL: Repeat old satire, Mort. It's just as funny and relevant as it was the first time....plus now, it's also prescient. Most of today's audiences won't even know the material is reruns....the best satire of all.

MORT: Sounds good, Paul. Let's go for it.

PAUL: Hey. Love, Peace and Holy Shit. Say goodnight, Gracie.

MORT: Goodnight, Gracie.

B

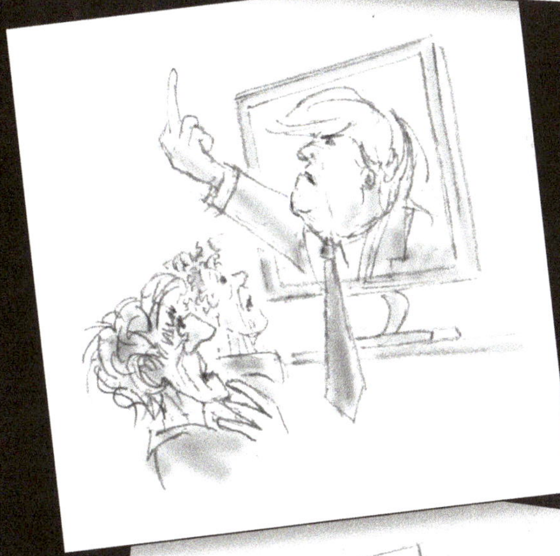

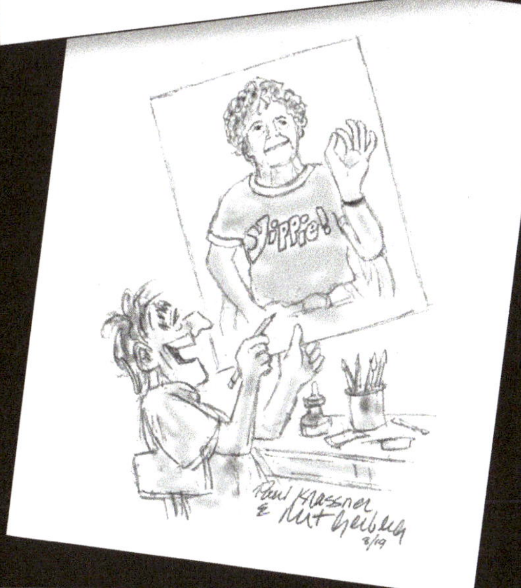
Yippie!
Paul Krassner & Mort Gerberg

MORT GERBERG *(@mortgerberg) is a multigenre cartoonist best known for work in* **The New Yorker**, et al., *including* **The Realist**, *and his book,* **Cartooning: The Art and the Business**.

PAUL KRASSNER *(1932-2019) was a journalist, comedian, editor, founding member of the Yippies, and one-time publisher of* **Hustler**. *He was, without doubt, the preeminent satirist of his generation.*

Gallimaufry

"A serious and good philosophical work
could be written consisting entirely of jokes."
Ludwig Wittgenstein

OTHER FIELDS, OTHER DREAMS.

When the voice came to Iowa, Ray Kinsella was not the only one to hear it.

Ray Firbin was in his basement, taping extra Thinsulate on the water heater, when he heard it. "If you build it, he will come."

Firbin consulted with his wife, and in a matter of three days he had torn out the drywall on one side to expose a brick wall, built a tiny stage, added some poor lighting and a few tiny tables out front that were constantly wet for some reason, and waited. At nine o'clock Friday night the spirits of Lenny Bruce, Joan Rivers, and George Burns showed up, did a solid ten, then sat in the back and compared the sandwiches they regretted ordering from Firbin's kitchen. Saturdays it was Richard Pryor, Rodney Dangerfield, Mitch Hedberg, and either George Carlin or Gary Shandling, depending who was in town. Robin Williams would pop unexpectedly to test new material. The crowds came from miles around. Then Louis CK showed up and ruined the whole thing and Ray Firbin turned it into a Samuel Beckett black box theater, which was not so popular.

◆

Ray Gaetana was fertilizing his soy crop when he heard the voice. "If you build it, he will come." His wife Cathy, skeptical by nature, suggested he record the voice next time he heard it. This Ray did. On the recording, Cathy could very plainly hear the whisper.

"What does it mean, Ray?," she asked.

"I don't know," he admitted.

They stared at the iPhone for some time. They played the simple message over and over, growing moody as red dusk descended on the long fields beyond the window. Finally Ray said, "You know, maybe if I had made a better recording..."

"Yes," said Cathy. "There's a lot of hiss on this thing. And the distortion on the lower band is almost embarrassing. I bet Ray Harrison could have filtered that out. Or Ray Morehouse, with the twenty-four band equalizer on his Bose portable? I bet that would have been great."

"The problem is the acoustics in that tractor cabin." A light came into his eyes slowly, like a wick catching in a hurricane lamp. "You know," said Ray Gaetana to his wife, "I bet, if I cannibalize the sound and generator systems in that ol' tractor, I could repurpose the chicken coop into a pretty enviable recording studio. We can put the chickens in the kids' room."

And thus did the ghost of Leopold Stokowski come to Churdan, off Route 4 just east of the Raccoon River. After several weeks complaining about the deal Disney had given him on Fantasia, he settled in to preparing an orchestral arrangement of "Popcorn," a number he said he had come to appreciate on the Other Side. Sure enough, after a week the ghosts of famous dead musicians started to fill the maestro's orchestra: Mozart on piano, Pablo Casals on viola, Harpo Marx on harp.

And there, in the back, polishing his xylophone, looking clean and sharp and smart in his tuxedo, was Ray Gaetana's father Earl.

Ray remembered, guiltily, the bitter argument he'd had with his father just before running away from home to attend William & Mary on an international law scholarship—the argument that had ended when Ray stormed out of the house with these closing words: "And another thing, Dad, I always hated playing the xylophone in the school band—I felt like an idiot in front of those cheerleaders!"

Ray now touched Cathy's hand as she stood by his side; Cathy, who had been a cheerleader. Ray joined his father at the xylophone. They did a duet of "Lady of Spain." Maestro Stokowski fired them.

"Is this Heaven, son?" asked the ghost of Earl Gaetana.

"No, Dad," said Ray. "In Heaven, nobody gets fired."

◆

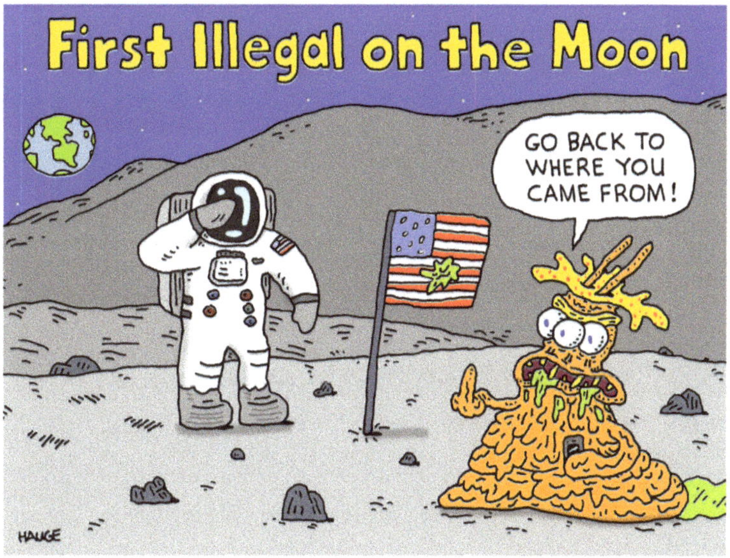
First Illegal on the Moon
GO BACK TO WHERE YOU CAME FROM!
HAUGE

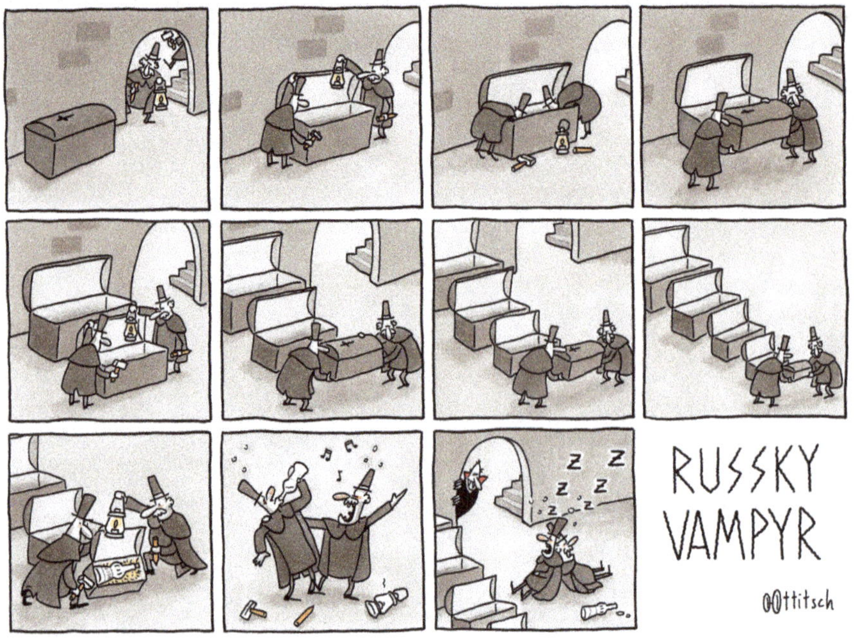
RUSSKY
VAMPYR
Ottitsch

The one unhappy story was that of Ray Coetzee, of Cedar Rapids, on the 2400 block of Halcyon Road, next to the airport on Englewood Road SW. "If you build it, he will come."

Mr. Coetzee, who had just been reading a coffeetable book on golf legend Ben Hogan, felt compelled to buy up sixteen houses in his neighborhood, plus Runway 9. He borrowed money from his brother-in-law Ray Firbin, who was feeling rather generous, having finally met his personal hero, the late great Bernie Mac. Coetzee built a regulation eighteen-hole golf course. He designed it himself. He did all the work himself.

When Ben Hogan finally showed up, he took one look and said, "This is the worst-designed course I've ever seen." Then he climbed out of the golf cart, and disappeared at the edge of the twelfth hole bunker.

Some weeks later the ghosts of Eisenhower and Bing Crosby began putting practice. When Ray asked them what they thought of the course, they changed the subject, but in a nice way.

Ray's youngest, Felice, said, "People will come, Daddy." And they did, but mostly hung out in the Ninth Hole Club, where Ray's wife June had taken a job as bartender. Half of these people were there because it was close to the airport, yet cheaper than the terminal bar.

No ghosts from Ray Coetzee's past ever appeared; he had always tried to stay on good terms with everybody, especially his immediate family. Eventually he sold the whole thing to a developer, who put up condos.

"Don't know what I was thinking of," he told people later. "I'd rather not talk about it."

—Walt Maguire

MEET THE NEW SUPERFOOD!

Meet the new superfood! Spit out your current food. Spit it onto a plate, or the ground, or wherever. Immediately. If that means spitting food on a loved one, make up with them later. Right now you're meeting the new superfood—and you're meeting it hard.

Move over, quinoa. Buzz off, açai. Leave us alone, Icelandic skyr, or we will tell this bar's bouncer his intuition is right and yes you are bothering us. We are in a serious, committed, hardcore relationship with the new superfood. We are kissing the old superfood goodbye. Also that kiss goodbye is an air kiss, because these lips only touch 100% Grade-A new superfood. And yes: these lips touch it with lots of tongue.

Have you experienced the all-natural borderline-illegal energy packed into the new superfood? It's the perfect superfuel! For a shopping trip to buy the new superfood!

As we all know, "food" is a corporate plot to give us too much cancer to be good parents. Yikes! Good thing science discovered the new superfood two seconds ago. Good thing the new superfood is nature's million-year-old miracle, helping generations of foreign people never die. Good thing we're taking everything in our pantry and chucking it into the city dump (where it feeds shorebirds -- great job!). Because if the new superfood ever met those old "foods," it would beat them up in front of your kids.

RESEARCH PROVES IT: the new superfood is your kids' new dad.

Bread. Dairy. Kale frittatas. These are a few of the "classic Food Pyramid food groups" we're saying goodbye to. We're saying goodbye to them because the new superfood kidnapped them, executed them, and threw them down an abandoned bauxite mine where their bodies will never be found. We know, we know: that sounds a little excessive. But isn't your health worth it? And also: if you say that one more time, the new superfood will turn kaij -sized and stomp Midtown.

The new superfood also tastes great in a smoothie!

Maybe you think you're not ready. Maybe you think you can't handle a new superfood that achieves The Singulari-Food and causes levitation during sex. Well guess what: the new superfood is sweeping the nation, and it's removed the word "maybe" from your vocabulary. It also removed unnecessary letters from our nation's name (Less Letters, Less Calories™). You're welcome, Amera! And finally forget all this because the new new superfood is eggs.

—Alex Schmidt

MISTAKES I'VE MADE.

While working craft services on the set of *Raiders of the Lost Ark* I decided to serve Harrison Ford a shish-kabob made from camel meat, not knowing how allergic he was to the stuff. As a result, the elaborate whip vs. sword battle which was to be filmed that day had to be scrapped, as did the scene where he rides a living camel off into the sunset. Sometimes I wonder how the movie turned out, but then I remember that I work in the movie industry and don't want to mix business with pleasure.

Once when a good friend of mine was about to be hanged for cattle rustlin' I gave him a slow wink and brushed my nose with my index finger, all whilst maintaining eye contact with him. I realized after he was successfully hanged that he might have mistaken my actions to imply a rescue was underway, when in fact I just wanted him to know that I was grateful for the time he shared his HBO GO login info with me.

Back in 1998 I had $5k to invest in the market. A friend gave me a tip that Apple was going to be the big stock of the new millennium, but instead I invested it in a company that promised to prevent 9/11 from happening. When 9/11 happened, the stock tanked and I lost almost everything.

My aunt Magnus Carlsen (not the chess champ, but she looks just like him) gifted me with a beautiful fridge magnet which I lost when I had to sell my fridge and forgot to remove all the magnets first. In my eagerness to regain my magnet I filled the atmosphere with iron filings, hoping that they would lead me to Magnus's magnet. Alas, they merely blotted out the sun, ushering in the ice age which destroyed human civilization as well as the need for fridges. I would say that this all ended like an O'Henry story, except no one reading this will know who O'Henry was, or really anything except how to hunt and catch a jellyfish off the coast of New Manhattan.

—*David Etkin*

YOUR WOMAN WANTS IT BIGGER.

To: Jim Harper
From: Morris Medicines, Inc.
Do not delete!! This is top important email to be delivered. Purchase 100% natural pills from doctors with framed awards. Make her happiest of all females by supersized penis. Give your woman the wants.
To: Morris Medicines, Inc.
From: Jim Harper
I had no idea my woman wanted it bigger. We've been having some problems (one of whom is named Chad), but this could save our marriage. How do I get these pills?
To: Jim
From: Morris
Thank you for taking together this opportunity for the most actual manliness. Please add Important Informations requested below for payment of $10000 USD.
To: Morris
From: Jim
Holy smokes! If I had $10,000 to spend on penis pills, I could pay anyone to love me. We're on a budget due to increasing expenses (public investigator for me, weekly STI testing for her). What can you do for $500 and a 4-star review?
To: Jim
From: Morris
You exhaust your woman with sameness. Take 750mg for all the days and your woman will accept addiction to pleasure.
To: Morris
From: Jim
Wait, what if she decides she wants it smaller? Jessy changes on a freakin' dime. For example: she used to love her ex-husband Arturo, then she loved me, and now she says she loves Chad.
To: Jim
From: Morris
No refunds if discover lack of pleasure from pills.
To: Morris
From: Jim
Don't worry, I'm still interested—I just worry that this, like everything else I do, won't make her happy. I bought a leather jacket, lost half my body weight, got a time-share in Lake of the Ozarks ($$$), bulked back up to my original body weight, and...nothing. Icy.
To: Jim
From: Morris
Your woman suffers from your lack of penis. We have scientific trials. I am offering results with images for proof of man.
To: Morris
From: Jim
Thank you for the photos. Those are... large. You know what I thought when I saw #3? "I'd have to wear a lifter's belt!" But if this is what my woman wants, this is what she shall have. Chad bought my custody rights which should cover the cost of the pills. (Apparently, he's also got it bigger in the banking arena.) I'll wire the money now.
To: Jim
From: Morris
You create admirable choices. Side effects contain immeasurable pleasure, infertility by option, kidney abandonment, silent death in sleep.
Four months later...
Morris Medicines Made Me a New Man...
4 Stars
A review by Jim
My penis has tripled in size, and so has my confidence. Before surprising my wife with the results, I flat-out asked her if she wanted it bigger. You know what she said? "No, I don't want it bigger. I

"Are we celebrating or sad? Either way I brought the wine!"

HOT DOGS I'LL BE SERVING AT MY CHARITY PICNIC

by Ben Doyle & Sandra Moore

A Hot Dog that is Very Small, Served on a Plate that is Very Large

A Hot Dog that has been Thoughtfully Rearranged

A Hot Dog that has been Thoughtlessly Rearranged

A Hot Dog that has been Served Within 25 ft. of Actor George Clooney

want a divorce." But I'm still taking the pills… this time for me. (Lifter's belt not included.)

—Lydia Oxenham

IN THE MORNING.

My favorite part of the day is in the barest sliver of a morning, when I wake up and find you beside me, still asleep. I carefully slip out of bed without disturbing you and tiptoe downstairs, avoiding every creaky floorboard, to make you breakfast.

I make you scrambled eggs, just the way you like them. Fluffy, with some green onions, covered in freshly-shredded cheddar cheese, with a couple cranks of black pepper. Then I sneak back upstairs and carefully balance the plate of eggs on the front of your face — so that when you wake up, the eggs will slide right into your mouth.

I do this because I love you.

Then, I go through the house and disable all the traps I had arranged the night before. Our house has, once again, made it through the night un-burgled, and the thought that I have kept you safe warms me. I take down the bucket of tar that I had precariously balanced above the door to the garage, disconnect the tripwire connected to the fan, and remove the plate of feathers from in front of the fan, dumping them back into a big sack that says "FEATHERS." Once the sack is full of feathers again, I put a pillowcase on it, and voila: I've made a pillow. I remove the dummies I had positioned all over our living room, attached to wires and pulleys to make it look as if they were practicing kung fu long into the night. Burglars who saw those dummies probably thought, "Well, we better not rob this house. It's filled with dummies who have come to life and learned the art of kung fu. Crane style kung fu, in fact—the most vicious and effective form." Little do those burglars know that the only people in the house were us, in the bedroom, cuddling.

As the sun is peeking its head out above the hills, a thin bright line starting to crest, I disable the last trap and put the anvil back in the attic. "Why do I keep the anvil in the attic?" I think every morning. But I know why I do it: Because I love you.

Now I make your lunch, so that when you are at your job, during the middle of the day when people generally get hungry, you can go to the office fridge, open it up, and pull out a brown paper bag with your name written inside of a heart. You will neither go hungry nor unloved. I carefully make you your favorite type of sandwich: crunchy peanut butter, blackberry jam, and rye bread. I write you a simple note that says, "I love you," and I slip it inside the sandwich. I wrap the sandwich carefully in cellophane, place it inside the bag, fold over the top of the bag once, staple the top, attach a combination lock to the top of the paper bag so that no one else in the office can take your lunch, and leave it on the counter next to the door for you to grab on your way out.

Finally, it is fully morning, and you wake up. You come downstairs, wiping your face and carrying a broken plate, and ask me what I've been up to so far.

"Oh, nothing," I say. I pull the newspaper back up in front of my face, to hide my warm, knowing smile. I love you.

—Curtis Retherford

'GODFATHER' CRIME FAMILY OR MAGGIANO'S MENU ITEM?

1. Tattaglia
2. Arrabbati
3. Barzini
4. Stracci
5. Marsala
6. Tilipia
7. Contadina
8. Cuneo
9. Manicotti

The Godfather: 1, 3, 4, 7
Maggliano Menu Item: 2, *also* 4, 5, 6, 8, 9

—Paul Lander

FIVE LIFE HACKS TO SAVE TIME AND DIGNITY

1. **Most people don't realize** that a little white vinegar can go a long way in the battle against household chores. First, invest in a gallon jug of the stuff from your favorite local grocer, and

then drink approximately three cups a day. You'll be shocked at how quickly getting stains off your windows drops in your list of priorities. For a little extra muscle, add a few drops of dish liquid. No, this is not a suggestion to drink dish liquid! That would be harmful. Instead, put a drop on each finger and gently rub into your eyes. Did someone say something about chores? No chores to see here, because of how much it burns!

2. ***If your shoes smell,*** don't throw them in the trash! Instead place an entire box of tea bags in your shoes. Use the most expensive tea you can find, which can be ordered either from Japan or an artisan tea shop owned by an eccentric couple who've been together long enough to have met at the first Women's Suffrage march. After letting the shoes sit for a few days, boil a pitcher of water and fill it with the smelly tea bags. *Voila!* You no longer have to throw away your shoes and you've brewed a medicinal feet tea you can sell at a profit at tailgate parties. Pour the tea over ice for a cool refreshment, or simply pour directly into toilet.

3. ***Speaking of shoes***, are yours too tight? Invite over your closest friend with gout. After making them 3-7 margaritas and putting on *The English Patient*, submerge your tight shoes in water. While your guest is engrossed in the movie, work the tiny, wet shoes onto their bloated feet. This must be attempted only during *English Patient* love scenes, of which there are far too few for such a long movie (including one that has a bagpipe). Then leave the wet shoes on their swollen feet until the end of the movie, five hours later. When they awake, they'll say, "Hey, who put these tiny, wet shoes on my feet??" The friendship will be over, but your shoes will fit you now.

4. ***Do you have a jar*** you can't get open? Just use duct tape! Prepare several long strips of duct tape and then begin wrapping the strips around your hands. Be sure to wrap the tape tight enough that you can feel your blood fighting to make its way down to your fingers. Once you've completely covered one hand in tape, attempt to tape up your free hand as well. You should now have two stiff, rubbery, throbbing claws. With your tape claws, lift the jar and throw it as hard as you can against the ground. If the jar is glass, it will shatter, freeing its contents for you to eat. If it is plastic, you will have to light it on fire, which will be almost impossible with your tape claws. Mission accomplished.

5. ***Use a tennis ball*** to keep from misplacing your keys! This one's a game changer. Keep spare tennis balls in your usual spaces, like, your car, bedroom, and kitchen, so that next time you lose your keys, the vibrant green ball will remind you that they're probably in your locker at the tennis court, where you usually get super-distracted on account of the affair you're having with your tennis instructor. Mission accomplished!

—***Sarah Hutto***

100% COMFORT. 0% WEEVILS. GUARANTEED.

Here at Terrestrial Textile Collective, we pride ourselves on using natural materials from Mother Earth and operating as a company with passion and principles. That's why we're thrilled to release our new underwear line, WeeKill—carefully crafted to swaddle derrières in über-soft, 100% organic cotton plucked directly from the hungry mouths of despicable boll weevils.

SUPPORTED BY SCIENCE

Gynecologists everywhere recommend wearing 100% cotton underwear, and—by the transitive property—they 100% love WeeKill! While developing our product, we did some asking around, and two out of three doctors agreed that if they saw a dead boll weevil on the side of the road—large or small—they would not stop to provide a proper burial.

Three out of three doctors asked us to leave after we posed that question, because the mere mention of the boll weevil elicits such tremendous disgust. We were even turned away from a few medical offices when we tried to enter the buildings while yanking a shackled boll weevil by a teeny metal chain. See how Science shuns them?

RESPONSIBLY SOURCED ORGANIC COTTON

The entire line of WeeKill underwear is made with 100% organic cotton,

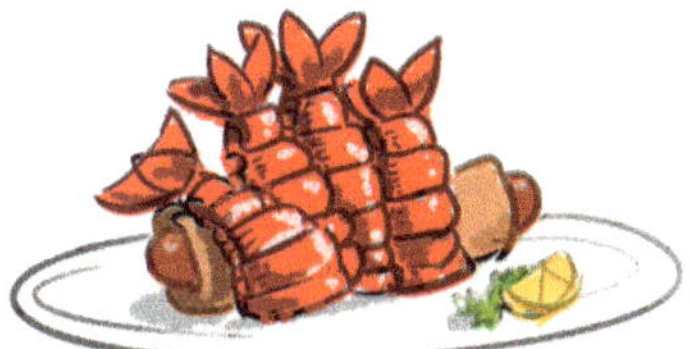

A Hot Dog that has been Hidden Behind a Modest Pile of Lobster Tails

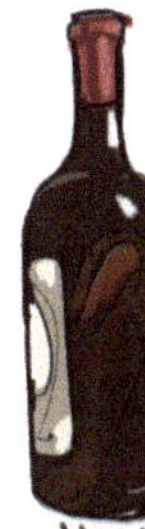

A Hot Dog that has been Served Inside a Bottle of 1928 Chateau Margaux

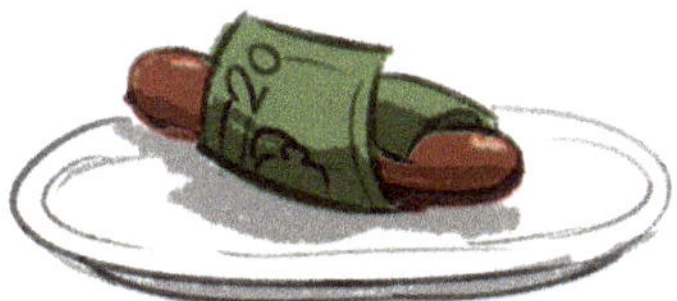
20

A Hot Dog that has been Served Inside a Crisp Twenty Dollar Bill

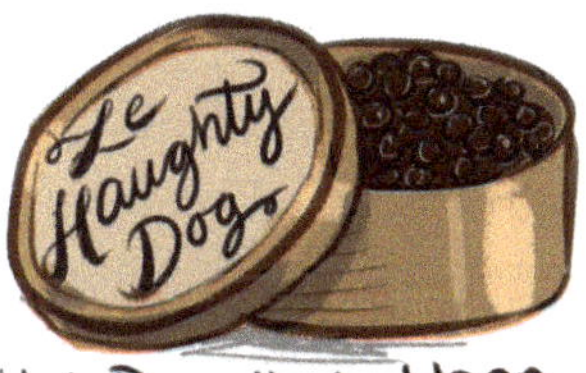
Le Haughty Dogs

A Hot Dog that, Upon Closer Inspection, is a Jar of Beluga Caviar

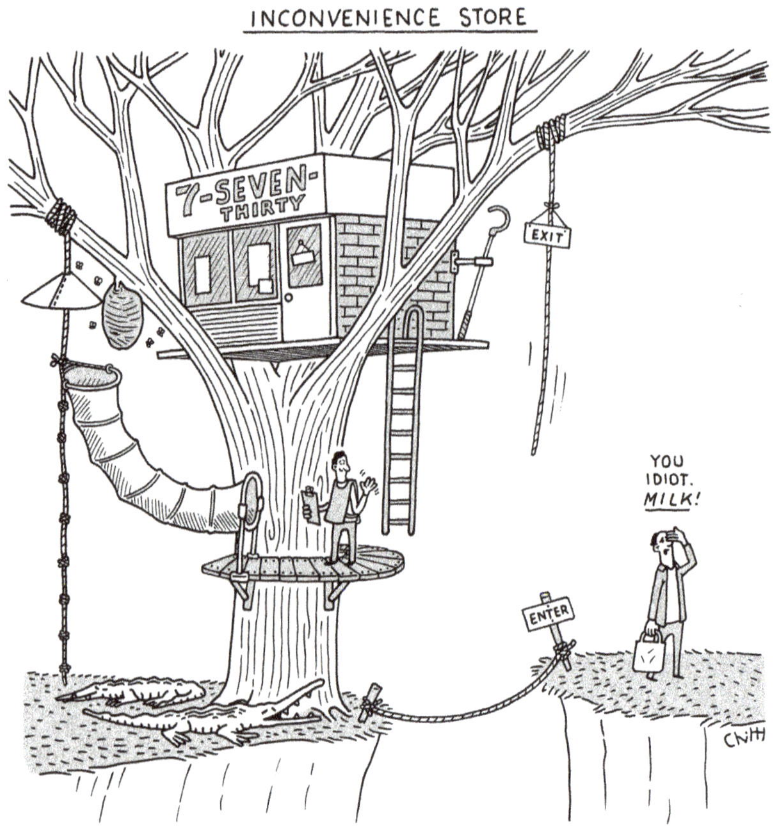
INCONVENIENCE STORE
7-SEVEN-THIRTY
EXIT
YOU IDIOT. MILK!
ENTER
CNTH

sourced responsibly. All of our cotton farmers are required to buddy up, hold hands, and not wander off. If that's not responsible, we don't know what is.

We're particular about the cotton we use for WeeKill underwear; most simply doesn't make the grade. It's got to be either getting slurped up the snout of a greedy boll weevil, or cotton that a boll weevil clearly had its eye on.

Raw cotton that's been snatched away from a boll weevil just feels better on your bottom. Trust us. Our entire staff rubbed two samples of raw cotton on our asses, and the nearly weeviled batch felt indefinably but unquestionably better. Still don't trust us? Give us a call and we'll put one of our asses on the phone to speak with you directly.

MINIMALLY PROCESSED

We like to keep things simple here at Terrestrial Textile Collective. Picture one of our farmers plucking a tuft of cotton out of the snout of a boll weevil, wiping off any weevil-spit, and then gingerly placing the tuft atop your genitals like a modesty cloud. Picture yourself smiling and flipping both middle fingers to the boll weevil you've deprived. Picture yourself saying out loud to the insect, "Your food source is now sheathing my genitalia. The cotton that was bound for your weird, elongated mouthpart has become a buffer garment for my anus."

That's the whole process in a nutshell! (Except for the farmer whacking the weevil with his weevil-whacking hoe. This is nonessential but fun.)

MADE WITH LOVE…AND HATE

Our underwear is made with deep love and reverence for our customers and the environment—and an unreasoning, unquenchable fury at *Anthonomus grandis* (you-know-who). Each member of the WeeKill team feels deeply personally fulfilled by the knowledge that our product will gently hug tushies and testes around the world, while draining the life-essence from boll weevils until they become listless, emaciated and eventually perish. Having this deep sense of purpose brings us immense joy, and we channel our joy into every pair of WeeKill undies.

"KILL THE WEEVIL." It's on every tag. Buy us wherever you buy fine underwear. Except if you're a weevil. Any weevils reading this can FUCK OFF!

—Cassidy Cummings

BAND NAMES THAT AT FIRST BLUSH SOUND TOUGH BUT UPON EXAMINATION, AREN'T.

Force of Habit
Dissociate
Tendency to Stutter
Ramping Up the Demand
Carbuncle
Ready to Brew
Pronounced Limp
Desist
Misconception
As Long As We're All Here, Let's Finish That Game of *Monopoly*

—Patrick Kennedy

STALIN, OFF THE DOME.

THE KREMLIN—*August 19, 1941*
Office of the General Secretary
Attendees: General Secretary Joseph Stalin; Lieutenant Sasha Apalkov

APALKOV: Comrade Stalin, I have news from the front. It's…not good.
STALIN: Tell me, lieutenant.
APALKOV: With the new German counterattack on the Volga, hundreds of thousands of our troops have perished. General Staff believes that this brings this year's total into the millions.
STALIN: Wow. It's really hard to comprehend death and loss when the numbers are on that scale. Which is pretty weird, considering that it's so sad when someone you know personally dies.
APALKOV: Indeed.
STALIN: It's almost like a single death is a tragedy, but a million deaths is a statistic.
APALKOV: Holy. Fucking. SHIT, comrade. Who originally said that?
STALIN: Oh, umm…maybe I just came up with it? Is that possible? Because woooow did I feel cool as shit saying it.
APALKOV: Honestly it's insane that one person can just come up with something so fucking awesome sounding, right off the dome.
STALIN: It's on the "I Came, I Saw, I

Conquered" level, right?? Like history books are going to record that I said that??...Look at my hands, Apalkov! I'm still shaking from how supremely kickass that line was! "One death is a tragedy! One million deaths is a statistic!" Wait, did I say "a single death" or "one death"?

APALKOV: I believe you said "a single death."

STALIN: Which is better? This is going to go down in history so I really want to nail it.

APALKOV: You only get to say a quote once. You can't go back and punch it up.

STALIN: But technically, if no one has said it either way, I'm the first to say it both ways.

APALKOV: Right, but you and I will know it was workshopped.

STALIN: I like the parallelism of the "ONE death" and "ONE million death", so I'll just say it that way to someone else and cut you out of the process entirely. I was going to purge you soon anyway.

APALKOV: That's cold, comrade.

STALIN: Well, I'm Stalin. Yolkov! Get in here.

Minister Yolkov is now present.

STALIN: I was thinking recently, and you know what? "One death is a tragedy; one million deaths is a statistic."

YOLKOV: Jeeeeeeesus Effing Christ that is one cool ass turn o' phrase, comrade! Who said that?

STALIN: I did! It came to me organically in that form, just now, right Apalkov?

APALKOV: Whatever you say, comrade.

YOLKOV: So you just blurted it out apropos of nothing?

APALKOV: Comrade Stalin, if I may, I think the quote hits harder with the appropriate context.

STALIN: Ah shit, you're right. Gotta do it again. Yolkov, you're dismissed. Please go shoot yourself twice in the back of the neck.

YOLKOV: Very good, Comrade Stalin.

Minister Yolkov has exited.

STALIN: Apalkov, is Budayev out in the hall?

APALKOV: Purged last week.

STALIN: Veselov?

APALKOV: Ooh, so close. Purged just this morning.

STALIN: Well just grab anyone then!

APALKOV: Here is young Yemelin. He cleans the bathrooms.

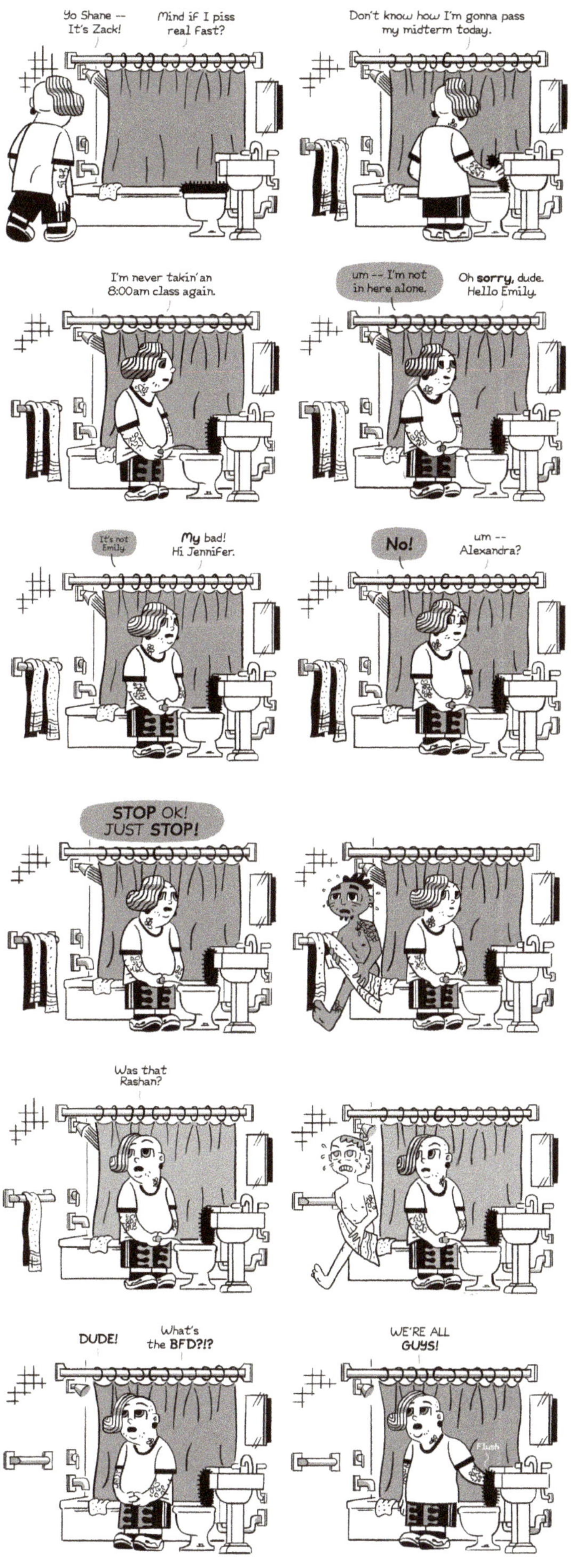

Yo Shane -- It's Zack!
Mind if I piss real fast?
Don't know how I'm gonna pass my midterm today.
I'm never takin' an 8:00am class again.
um -- I'm not in here alone.
Oh sorry, dude. Hello Emily.
It's not Emily.
My bad! Hi Jennifer.
No!
um -- Alexandra?
STOP OK! JUST STOP!
Was that Rashan?
DUDE!
What's the BFD?!?
WE'RE ALL GUYS!
Flush

ART BAXTER

STALIN: Have him read the report you read to me five minutes ago.
YEMELIN: I can't read, Comrade Stalin. You purged my parents—and all the teachers—
STALIN: Apalkov, for Christ's, who I don't believe in, sake, please whisper the information into his ear, so he can then repeat it to me.
APALKOV: Very well. [inaudible whispering]
YEMELIN: "Comrade Stalin, hundreds of thousands of—"
APALKOV: No, no, you don't need to mimic my voice. Just do it as you.
YEMELIN: OK, sorry. "Comrade Stalin, hundre—"
STALIN: "One death is a tragedy; one million deaths is a statistic!"
YEMELIN: Wowowowow holy shit that is a very badass thing to shout, Comrade Stalin! What's it from?
STALIN: It just came to me, just now, in exactly that phrasing.
YEMELIN: Well, it's very you.
STALIN: Thanks! Yemelin, stay for a drink to celebrate my getting into Bartlett's. Apalkov, you do think I'll —
APALKOV: Oh for sure.
YEMELIN: Sorry, I can't stay. Someone self-purged in the bathroom this morning and I need to clean it up before it starts to smell.
STALIN: Well it's like I always say: One mess is a tragedy; one million messes is a statistic.
YEMELIN: Not as good.
STALIN: They can't all be winners. I'm talking all day! Luckily History will never know I said it, unless for some reason the transcript my secretary is typing at this very moment is published in the future, detailing this exact conversation.
YEMELIN: Can't imagine that would ever happen, comrade.
STALIN: Nor can I.
APALKOV: The problem with that 'messes' version is that it feels derivative.
STALIN: Yes, we know that, Apalkov. You didn't have to say it.
APALKOV: Apologies, comrade.
STALIN: God, I can't wait to purge you.

—Matt Powers

WINE NOT?

Hey there Oenophiles! Trevor here with another *cab*-ulous Wine Social newsletter for your *zin*-box! First, a re-*vine*-der to join us at Not Too Chablis on Ventura Boulevard this Friday at 8pm when Mitzi from Cerro Caliente will be pouring from their spring tasting menu. It's sure to be a *Grand Cru* in attendance, so *Semilon* down to sip with us! *Wine not??*

Now, a few of you have *casked* why you haven't heard from me *grapely*. I *blush*, but this is kind of *chard* to talk about...Things are *tokay* now, but life can really be a *brut*.

It happened while I was delivering the keynote at the World Of Wine Summit in Jacksonville. As I took the podium, a wave of pure *terroir* came over me. My mind went *blanc*. "*Demi-sec*," I said, trying to focus on my notes, hoping it would *Ripasso*, but it didn't. My *mouthfeel* dry, the room *turned* and it felt like I'd been shot in the gut at *Pinot Blanc* range. I'll be *Sancerre* with you...I thought I had one foot in the *Graves*.

Everything after my *spill* is a *blend*. I remember blood *pouring* out of my *nose* and someone saying "*Saint Emillon*, look at his eyes." Next thing I know, I'm waking up in a hospital room, scared and all a-*Rhone*. I had the most horrible nightmare—I was on a wine tasting weekend in the Finger Lakes. Just horrible. Then I realized... why *Chianti* feel my legs?! The doctors *swirled* in, each one *Mersault*-ing me with questions, "*Decant breathe*!" one shouted. "*Gamay* some space!" I said weakly. They gave me twenty minutes to *mellow*, so I could *open up* to what would truly be a *bottleshock*...when I came to the E.R., I was in bad shape—suffering from severe abdominal *maceration* and in desperate need of a new liver. Thankfully I come from a family of teetotalers and my mother *Rousanne* was a perfect match. I was put in a medically in-*juiced* coma and wheeled *vin*-to surgery. Nine out of *tannin* would have kicked the *bouquet*...but I was lucky. The procedure was a *sparkling* success. My wife, my kids, my parents —all had *clustered* around, wondering when I'd wake up from my *Napa*. They were practically dying of *Bordeaux*, I'm sure. :-)

That was eighteen quarterly wine shipments ago. Eighteen shipments spent in an inky blackness I would liken to a dark Douro Red. As delicious as that sounds, I wouldn't wish it on my *Gewurtz* enemy.

I won't lie, it's been a long road *Bacchus*. I want to *Reserva* special thanks to my physical therapist Gino, who helped me get back on my *stems*—sir, you are truly a *Super Tuscan*. And to the doctors on staff at Cedars, I'm in your *Muscadet*. I feel lucky most days, but *Cinsault* much time has passed. My dear *petite Syrah* moved on and paired with a *soave light-bodied Californian*. My kid *revisits* occasionally, but the only thing I hear from *Sherry* is, "YOU CAN'T *MUSCATEL* ME WHAT TO DO!" For a long time I looked for any *Port* in the storm. I tried religion, but they only have sacramental wine. Honestly, I felt

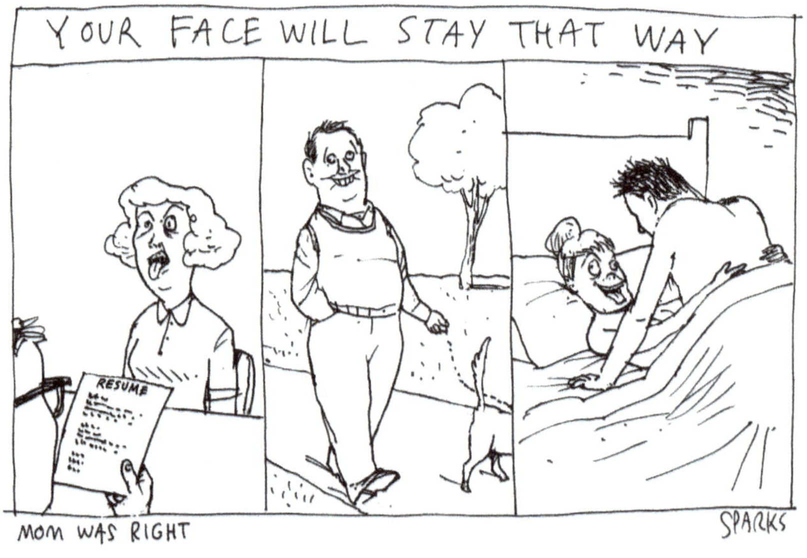
YOUR FACE WILL STAY THAT WAY
RESUME
MOM WAS RIGHT
SPARKS

like *grappa*. I missed out on the *peak* years of my life and what was left felt like too much to *Barbera*. All my good luck I *sauterne* to bad.

But then something happened. One day I just looked myself in the mirror and said, "Trevor, who do you think you're *Lagavulin*? You're not some withering thing, dying on the vine. A little bad luck isn't going *tequila*—you're strong, spirited and living *proof* that it's blue *Skyy* ahead! The future is *Dewar's*, *oaky*? So go out there and *Maker's Mark*!" After this long *absinthe*, I realize I've still got plenty of gas in the *Tanqueray* and the world is *Absolut* spinning with possibilities. So with that said, I'll be stepping away from the Wine Social newsletter. *Anejo*, *Anejo* — I'll miss you too. But, *Aperol* I've been through, I think you'll agree this is for the best. Maybe I'll be *Bacardi* someday, but on the *Smirnoff* chance I'm not... L'chaim!

—Lars Kenseth

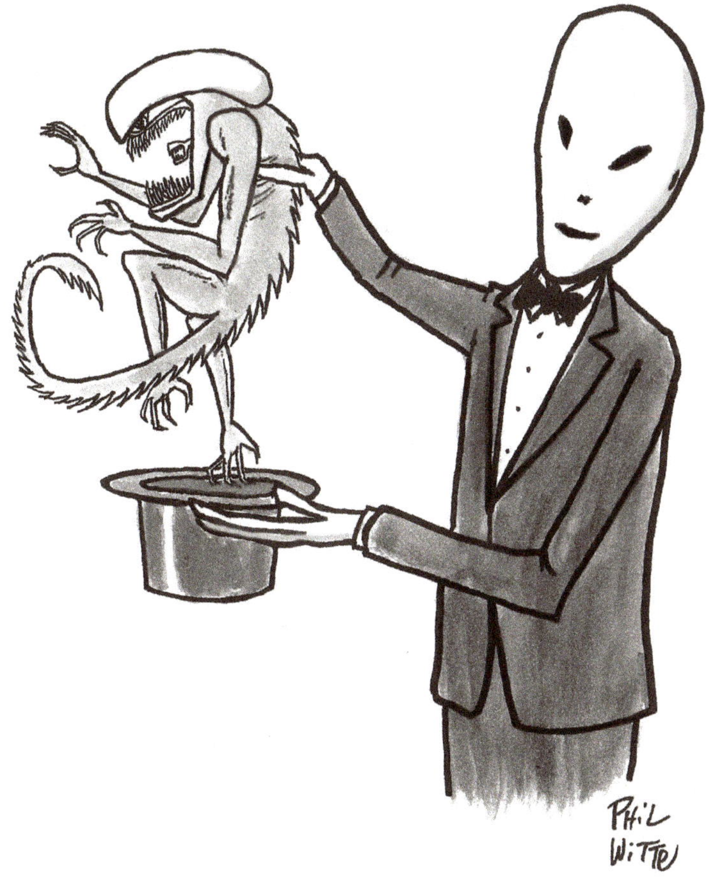
PHIL
WITTE

EVERYTHING'S DIFFERENT NOW.

On a recent flight from Dallas to LA, I was upgraded to a seat in First Class. It was a transformative experience.

During the "bad old days" in Economy, I held a definite grudge against those at the front of the plane. They seemed alien to me. Their seats transformed into luxurious beds. They drank mimosas. They seemed happy to fly. Several kilometers to the rear, surrounded by screaming infants and crumb-covered man-children playing first-person shooter games, my disdain was palpable.

Friends, I was ignorant. Things are different now. Now, I understand.

In First Class, I was finally surrounded by the type of people and service I require when traveling! This was immediately apparent when my seatmate (1B) flashed his perfect smile and introduced himself: "Keith Squires, Executive VP, Malingus Medical Sales."

Keith shook my hand with a fraternal squeeze, then offered me a cigar. (In First Class, cigar smoking is not only allowed, but encouraged, as long as it is a real Cuban.) Our flight attendant and former swimwear model arrived with a curtsy and lit my stogie.

"Welcome, gentlemen. I'm Gwen," she said. "I'm here to serve you and see that you are completely taken care of. Then, and only then, will I see to the safety of the other passengers."

Gwen handed us two invitations to a reception being held by a lovely young couple in 3D and 3E— Dominic and Dominique. We meandered over just as they opened an excellent 1990 Château Margaux. In no time we were reminiscing: Summer nights out on the Cape; which custom shotguns we would never be able to part with, even in death; the thrills of trading the volatile Japanese markets around the Christmas tree. Keith struck up "God Bless America" in his angelic tenor.

There was not a dry eye in the first six rows.

Did I mention that in First Class a hot towel is provided periodically throughout the flight? A hot towel! Unsure of what it was for, I blew my nose with mine and threw it on the floor. In a flash, Gwen was there, picking it up and replacing it with a new hot towel which I fashioned into a hot ascot.

Dinner was served. A perfectly seared fillet of Atlantic Salmon over fresh watercress, topped with scintillating conversation and the exchange of business cards.

I now believe—scratch that, I know it in my bones—that lower taxes on the wealthiest Americans are a good thing. The economics are simple: if we save more money, we will buy more first class tickets. More tickets means more money for the airlines. More money for airlines means more jobs. It's as plain as the hot ascot on your chest.

Speaking of trickle-down, dessert was treacle fit for Louis XVI. Simply scrumptious.

Yes, I say "scrumptious" now.

Keith and I were mulling over an aperitif when I felt a tap on my shoulder. It was my traveling companion (my wife), appearing rather pale and emaciated, and with a slightly haunted look. She had come forward to ask if I might spare any of my leftovers. I felt embarrassed in front of Keith. "My dear," I drawled, "was your salmon not filling enough?"

"What the hell are you talking about?! We don't get food in economy!" she said, grabbing a half-eaten dinner roll from my tray and storming off to who knows where.

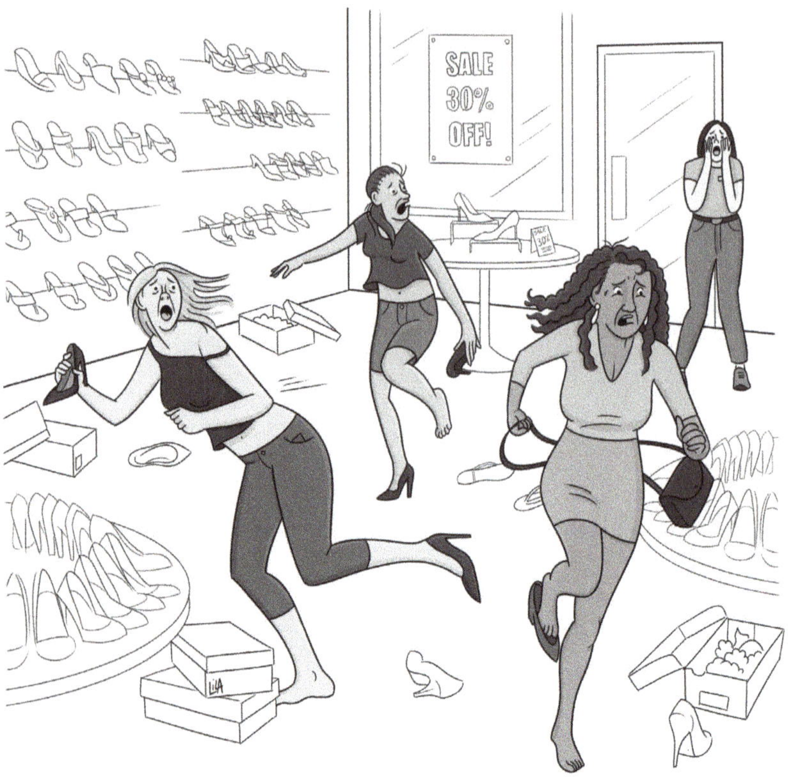
SALE
30%
OFF!

"Tarantino's here! Everybody run!"

As I watched her retreat, I realized I could no longer recall what Economy travel was like. It was then that Gwen, ever so politely, reminded me that under no circumstances were service items to be given to passengers not seated in First Class.

"Oh, I know darling!" (I also say "darling" now.) "The old girl just looked so damned hungry!"

We shared a good laugh before I demanded another hot towel to throw on the floor.

This is not to say First Class is without its hardships. At one point, I woke to find a woman and small child loitering in the aisle. I had never seen them before, and suspecting they were from …somewhere aft, I watched in horror as they attempted to use the First Class lavatory. The mother mumbled some gibberish about how all the other bathrooms were in use, and her son had a congenital malformation of the bladder causing severe pain and urgency with urination, or something.

Not seeing Gwen, I had no choice but to heroically stand in the aisle and block her way. I explained to this woman how hard I had worked to be able to use the First Class lavatory. If she could just work hard too, there would come a day when she might enjoy it as well. Her son had begun to hop up and down, and she scooped him up and ran for the back of the plane before I could finish telling her that if we all broke the rules, there would be no First Class, and it would be chaos.

As the plane descended, I looked around at my new friends. My god, I would miss them. I bid a tearful adieu to each one with three cheek kisses. How long would it be until we were all together again?

Thanks to Keith, and my new position as Executive Director of Malingus Medical Sales, I expect it won't be long at all. Cheers!

—Greg Hess

RULES FOR THE QUIET CAR.

Welcome aboard Amtrak's Northeast Corridor Express Quiet Car traveling from New York to Washington D.C. We have made this Quiet Car available for your comfort, convenience, and enjoyment. With that in mind, here are a few simple rules to make the journey as pleasant as possible for all aboard.

- Cell phone use is strictly prohibited in the Quiet Car.
- Please limit all conversations to zero.
- Sneezing, coughing, or other loud bodily events are not allowed in the Quiet Car. In case of illness, conductors can provide a flexible sound-dampening containment suit upon request.
- There is no laughter in the Quiet Car.
- Books, magazines, newspapers and other rowdy paper materials are strictly prohibited.
- Kindles and other E-readers are also strictly prohibited. Passengers who would like to read aboard the Quiet Car are encouraged to memorize a book of their choice and think about it quietly.
- Wearing loud materials (such as crinoline or cordoroy) is strictly prohibited.
- The Quiet Car should remain vacuum-sealed and empty at all times to retain its value and collectability.
- Cries for help are not allowed in the Quiet Car.
- Obviously, food or beverages are not permitted in the Quiet Car. This is especially true for that toasted chicken and avocado sandwich you bought at Au Bon Pain wrapped in material made from 100% recycled wind chimes.
- Seating in the Quiet Car is on a first-come, first-served basis. All seating disputes will be settled by silent combat inside our Murder Cage™ conveniently located on top of the train.
- Keep movement to a minimum. Sit up straight. Quietly place your hands on your knees and look forward, taking appropriate care to limit head movement to a minimum. No fidgeting. No twitching. No blinking.
- The Quiet Car can smell fear.
- If you encounter a Quiet Car in the wild, do not run. Avoid direct eye contact. Pepper spray is ineffective against a charging Quiet Car. Walk away slowly. When you have reached a safe distance, alert the proper authorities.
- The "t" in Quiet Car is silent. As are all the other letters. *As you should be.*

We hope you enjoy your time aboard Amtrak's Quiet Car. Not enjoying your time aboard Amtrak's Quiet Car is strictly prohibited.

Thank you for choosing Amtrak! Not choosing Amtrak is strictly prohibited.

—Kristopher Wood B

FROM FANTAGRAPHICS UNDERGROUND

A Fistful of Drawings

A Graphic Journal by Joe Ciardiello

A paean to Hollywood, a love letter to the Western, and a tribute to its Italian influences.

In this gorgeous graphic memoir, Joe Ciardiello gracefully weaves together his Italian family history and the mythology of the American West while paying homage to the classic movie and TV Westerns of the '50s and '60s. Featuring Ciardiello's signature sinuous ink line and vivid watercolors, *A Fistful of Drawings* illuminates the oversized characters that dominated the cinematic American West—Clint Eastwood John Ford, John Wayne, Claudia Cardinale, Sophia Loren, and many more.

A Fistful of Drawings
A Graphic Journal by Joe Ciardiello

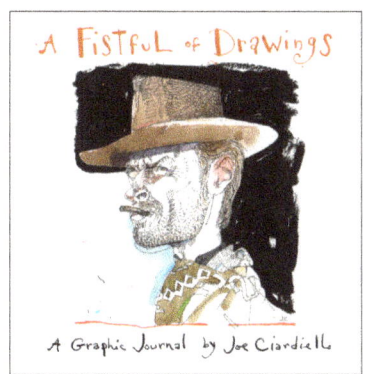

"Joe Ciardiello has been one of America's finest artists for the last generation. Here we finally have his magnum opus: a project that brilliantly blends mid-century culture, the Italian-American experience, and his own personal story into something rare in form, unique in content, and startlingly deep in every nuance. It is a work of genius."

—Steve Brodner
Illustrator/political satirist

Ciardiello
Claudia Cardinale

ORDER NOW AT FANTAGRAPHICS.COM

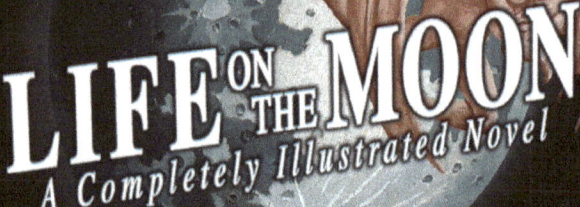

SECOND THOUGHTS
BY AL GORE

I WAS WRONG: THE ZOMBIE APOCALYPSE WILL KILL HUMANS BEFORE CLIMATE CHANGE

I have spoken around the world to warn my fellow inhabitants of this planet about the dangers of carbon emissions and the devastating effects of human-caused climate change. But I now believe our planet faces an even more imminent danger: a crazed swarm of flesh-eating zombies.

Let me be clear: climate change will likely be catastrophic if we do not act. Certainly sea levels will rise, we will see more droughts, and there will be an increase in wildfires. But it's time to forget all that. Zombies will chew your face off as soon as they catch you.

Climate change is happening at the slow pace of geological time. We know now that zombies, on the other hand, can burst through windows and break through doors and grab us and bite us to death in seconds.

I, along with many of our top zombie experts, now believe that any discussion of climate change and what we might do to stop it, is pointless. Recycling, clean energy, wind power—it's all a tremendous waste of time. Junior high-school students must put an end to their hopelessly naive Earth Day projects and cardboard dioramas for their school science fairs, and must instead run for their lives from the unspeakable evil that is the reanimated dead.

Zombies will not only ravage every man, woman and child on Earth—they will, once they bite you, cause you to transform bodily into the unholy living dead yourself. This is the existential threat zombies pose to humanity.

You see, once the bite of a zombie takes effect, we are not just dead. We are *undead*. And we strengthen their number, increasing their destructive power, hastening their vile desecration of all we hold sacred. Once we have been infected with the zombie curse, we will decompose, we will be rendered void of any emotional attachment to others, we will not recognize our loved ones, and we will seek only to devour their brains to feed our senseless zombie rampage.

We are already seeing the effects of the zombie apocalypse. The dreadful creatures are already upon us, their arms outstretched, their bodies reeking of rotting flesh.

I myself have faced zombies. Just the other day I was chased by a horde of the screeching monsters after my family and I had taken shelter in an abandoned farm house. While my wife Tipper and I escaped, sadly, the zombies consumed my son, Al, Jr., and he became one of them.

You can understand, then, that this issue is a deeply personal one for me. I then had to make the most agonizing decision that I have ever had to make as a father. I had to blow my son's head off.

I now consider it my top priority to educate the entire human race, to do what I can to prevent any other father from having to make the same terrible choice.

We know the solution. We have known it a long time, but powerful zombies and their unearthly screams have only sown confusion. They deny the pending disaster, while at the same time contributing to the problem by relentlessly overrunning the living and poisoning our blood. When I met with leading zombie scientists recently in Oslo, their message could not have been more clear. They said, simply, *"Brains!"*

We must listen to the zombies. Their most prominent thinkers are telling us exactly the course we must take to mitigate the effects of the looming zombie apocalypse. In short, we can stop them only with violent head trauma. *We must destroy their brains.*

We must all do our part to take this meaningful action. You can fire your shotgun at the head of a zombie and shatter its brain and kill it. I know this first-hand. You can also slice a zombie's head clean off with a machete, sword, or shovel. In addition, their heads can be crushed, burned, or sawed off. Every little bit helps.

Every home in our country must be retrofitted with decapitation-grade weaponry for this purpose.

I have sent a letter to President Trump warning him of the seriousness of this issue, and outlining the simple steps we must take to save our planet from the zombies. I have sent similar letters to other world leaders, the heads of universities, and other academic and scientific institutions.

But no one is listening.

That is why I have come directly to you, the citizenry of this planet. My warning is stern and heartfelt: *kill the zombies*.

Join me as I roam the Earth, my bolt-action shotgun slung over my shoulder, on an obsessive quest to annihilate as many of these ungodly walking corpses as I am able. Muddied and tattered from my tireless, one-man battle, I rest fitfully when I can, silently ceding to my fate as the savior of all humanity.

SCOTT DIKKERS is The Onion's *longest-serving editor in chief and the #1* New York Times *best-selling author of* How to Write Funny. *He's also the founder and editor of* Blaffo Magazine *(www.blaffo.com).*

MICROSTARS

BY ROY BLOUNT, JR.

TEN INCREDIBLY SHORT PEOPLE YOU DIDN'T KNOW WERE CELEBRITIES

They may not be the faces that you literally cannot watch TV without seeing pop up all the time, but they're out there in the celebrisphere, and how much less than normal height they are? You have no idea.

1. *Get Tha Hook/Seattle* co-host **Dylis Bison** would like people to know that she has a caring side. This came to light when her barely-clad cry from the heart, meant only for the eyes of a few, went near-viral. From any side, she is virtually minuscule.

2. Among themselves, celebs will say—and do?!—just about anything, but they'll never, ever bring up how typical their lack of height is. Yet **Mel Derwent** of *Real People of South Carolina* is perhaps best known for being incredibly short even for a celebrity. Mel was barely five feet in CGI heels when, unfortunately, he died, leaving an unforeseen void.

3. Due to an inherited syndrome, **Cissy Piers** starts the day at five-foot-five-and-a-half, but loses an inch, on average, with every waking hour. Unsurprisingly, this equates to wardrobe issues. Example: seven different onesies for a long day's shoot on *Whoops, We're Babies!* (She's uncredited.)

4. **Umi Pumi**. Nothing about him looks famous, and this troubled son-of-refugees has been called "faceless," to boot, but ask any other celeb if they know Umi and here's what you'll hear: "Umi? Little short guy?"

5. **Gavin Hoke-Ixley** may not be *short*-short. Just slightly under average height for non-celebrities (if they are British). But those who know say he looks shorter next to his several cats, for instance, than you'd think. He was the lickspittle on *Crosley Harrows*.

6. Last year **Margo Pom** was voted least-visually-recognized celebrity having a copyrighted catch-phrase ("Oh, c-c-c-come on"). Celebrity analysts point to her real-life height: well below average-eye-level.

7, 8. **"The Phelpses"**? The famous next-door neighbors of the Pine Bluff Nugents on season four of *Next-Door Neighbors From Hell*? Not the McMonikers, the ones from Hell, but the nice neighbors on the other side that the Nugents were always wishing, "If only the McMonikers were more like the Phelpses!"? So—that really tiny couple you would see sometimes scooting past the house and not waving? That's them, **"the Phelpses."** Perhaps for size reasons, **"the Phelpses"** (not their real names) declined to take part in the series voluntarily. Their real name is Ghent.

9. Tall early on, **Kemper Org of Org.com** doesn't mind revealing he could beat up anybody, and did, until fourth grade, when his growth unexpectedly stopped. He credits this, he tells insiders, as his original motivation to win a place among the famous. He can beat plenty of them up. And so could you.

10. This will make your head explode: **your Uncle Chip**. That's right, the Chipmeister is way known in certain circles which he would totally do anything to keep you from conveying to your Aunt Felice. And we don't have to tell you how short the Chipster is.

MORE FOR YOU FROM AROUND THE WEB:

- *Ear-Stubble: Lose It, or Use It?*
- *5 Amazing Secrets to Reduce Your Unsightly Flab*
- *Why Don't More People Grow to Resemble Their Cats?*

COMMENTS:

Mary_Worth: "Why can't we move on past height size? Because a person is short doesn't mean they are a certain way. It is just a number. It doesn't make them any more or less of a person."

T. Archer: "How would you get in touch with them? If you would even want to. Perhaps the most unbelievable thing about them, they seem to want you to believe they care about you even less than you do about them."

Mg Mg Vwe: "A truly interesting facts of celebrities. We do not in Sri Lanka." **B**

ROY BLOUNT, JR. *is about as tall as you'd think, except from the side. He is listed on Wikipedia under 'American humorists' and 'American rock musicians.' The latter listing is undeserved.*

BARRY BLITT

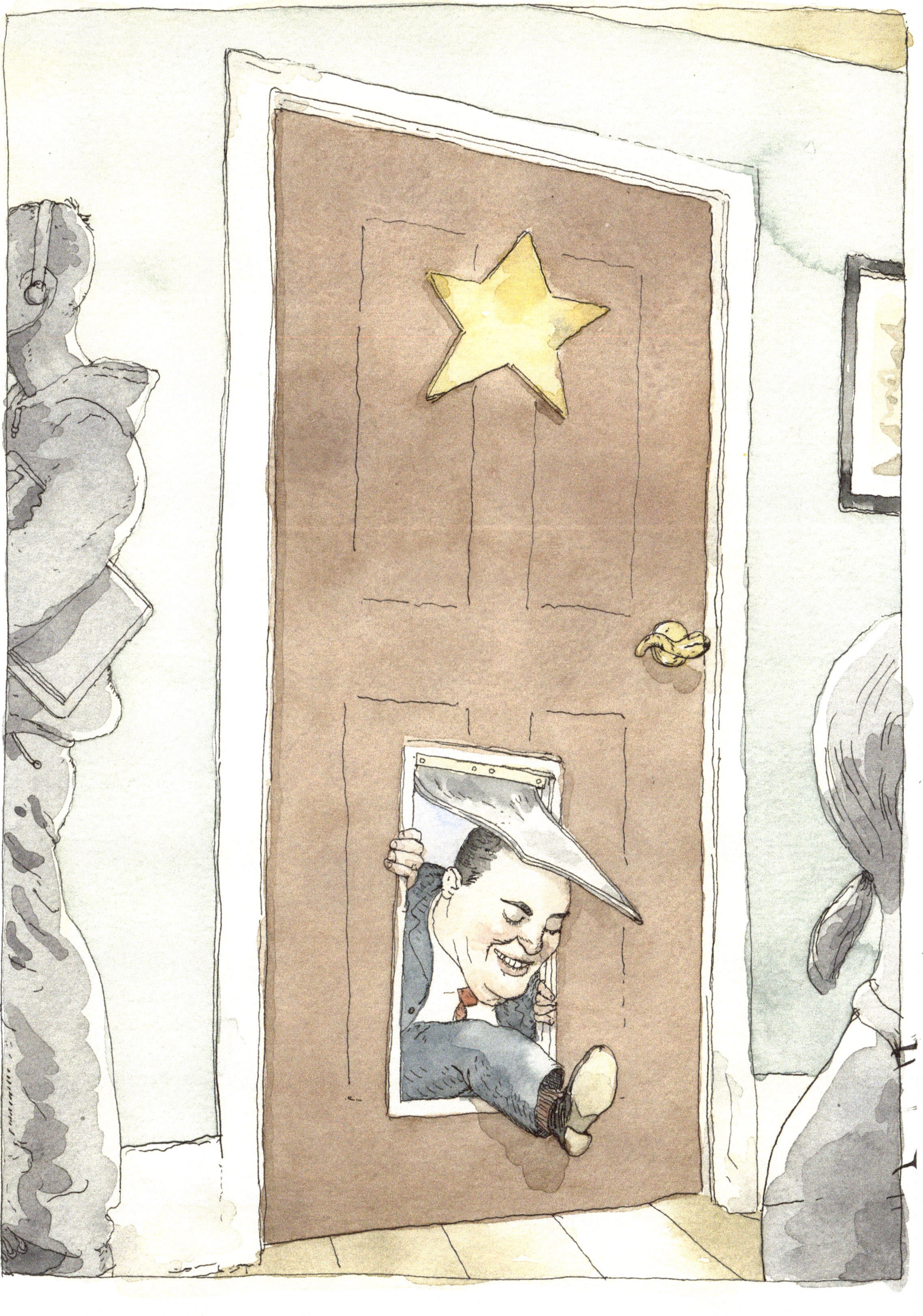

A STATEMENT
BY JENNIFER KIM

I AM AN ARTIST
Answering the "why" questions

I am an artist.

I paint on any surface I find, including my neighbor's back patio. Because the world is my canvas and I am doing something brave and real. And when my neighbor knocks on my door to confront me, I hide in my pantry and pretend not to be home. That is part of it.

It is difficult to be an artist like me because I am not popular amongst the youths and I am not popular amongst the adults. Also, I am not popular.

I carry around a pencil in my hair at all times because you never know when inspiration might strike. The downside to this is that my hair is filled with pencils.

I would like to collaborate with other people. But they would not like to collaborate with me. Something about how at the last "wine and cheese mixer" I "took my pants off" and told everyone their art was "derivative" and "lame" and that they were all "losers in my book!" I don't remember doing that and even if I did, it was probably some sort of performance art thing that I was doing.

It's hard to be an artist that pushes boundaries because not everyone understands my intentions. I get a lot of "why" questions. "Why are you doing this?" "Why would you take the time to repaint that entire gray wall in exactly the same color? It's gray still. You can't even tell that you did anything." "Why…sorry, I meant what is *wrong* with you?" And to those confused audience members, I ask you to not see the art for what it might be on the surface, but dig deeper. Because that piece is actually about racism. Now, think about why you didn't catch that.

I make art naked. Meaning, I am naked, and I order my assistant to go outside and make the art for me. Some say that this is cheating. I say, whose name is on that piece of art? Is it good? If it's good it's me and if it's bad, it's my assistant's.

It is difficult when you see the world in color and everyone else sees it in black and white. That is the artist's way. I guess it is also the way of a person who is not color-blind, hanging around a bunch of color-blind people. But are they good at painting fruits? Didn't think so.

Since it is hard for people to understand what I do and how creative I am, I like to wear my smock everywhere I go to show everyone up. Except sometimes, people think I'm a chef or a barbershop man or something instead. And to those people, it's like are you stupid or something?

And with that, I conclude my introduction. Again, welcome to my exhibition. Donations are accepted and strongly encouraged. You can also just give me cash right now if you want. I'd actually rather do that, let's do that.

JENNIFER KIM *(@kjenn32) is a comedy writer in Los Angeles. She has contributed to places like* **McSweeney's, Points in Case,** *and* **Little Old Lady Comedy.** *It is good!*

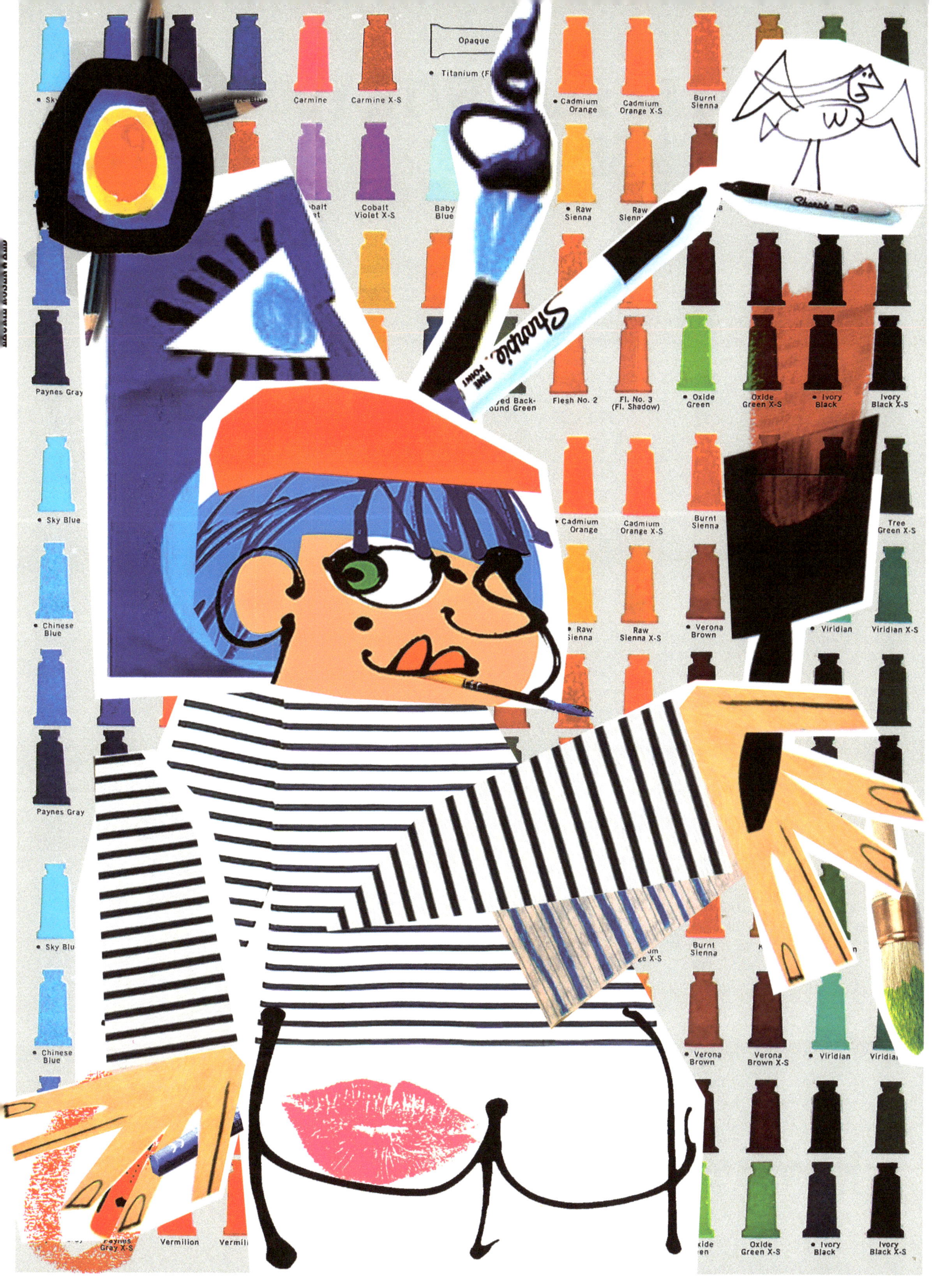
Opaque
Carmine
Carmine X-S
Cadmium Orange
Cadmium Orange X-S
Burnt Sienna
Cobalt Violet X-S
Baby Blue
Raw Sienna
Sharpie
FINE POINT
Paynes Gray
Flesh No. 2
Fl. No. 3 (Fl. Shadow)
Oxide Green
Oxide Green X-S
Ivory Black
Ivory Black X-S
Sky Blue
Cadmium Orange
Cadmium Orange X-S
Burnt Sienna
Tree Green X-S
Chinese Blue
Raw Sienna X-S
Verona Brown
Viridian
Viridian X-S
Paynes Gray
Burnt Sienna
Chinese Blue
Verona Brown
Verona Brown X-S
Viridian
Vermilion
Oxide Green X-S
Ivory Black
Ivory Black X-S

TRUTH BOMBS
BY YANKEE DOODLE

CAN I BE REAL WITH YOU FOR A SECOND?

I know I'm gonna get in trouble for saying it, but fucking "PC culture" is killing this business. Back in the day, you could get away with *anything* in the nursery rhyme world, so long as it was funny. Me, I'd do my famous routine where I'd stick a feather in my cap and call it macaroni.

And let me tell you: That shit fucking KILLED.

No matter where I performed, everyone was all, "Yankee Doodle, keep it up!" I'd get fucking mobbed, and I was always like, "Mind the music and the step, guys," but secretly, I fuckin' loved it. Even the girls, everyone was like, "With the girls be handy!" Just, you know, encouraging me—meanwhile, girls are just *hurling* themselves at me. You know why? Because that was during the golden fucking age of nursery rhymes. When you didn't have to be afraid of offending anyone.

You could take *risks*. Because that's what real nursery rhymes do. I coulda stuck a feather in my cap and called it anything—penne, linguine, mostaccioli—but that's playing it safe. Me, I just decided to go there, because I always say what everybody's thinking, but is AFRAID to say. So I thought, "Fuck it." And pointed to my cap and...well, you know the rest.

Can you imagine doing that routine at a college these days? I was talking to my good friend, the Farmer in the Dell, and he said, "Don't play colleges, they're so PC." He should know—he's got this whole "take my wife" bit where, you know, he takes a wife, that's just absolutely fucking hilarious. But does that kind of stuff play anymore? No.

I try to bring my whole macaroni thing to a college, and two seconds later I'm getting protested about not being sensitive to gluten-free or whatever. All the celiacs start shouting and walking out, and everybody else misses out on a brilliant bit. Is that fucking fair? You've got no sense of humor, fine, but don't *censor* me, dude. Fucking freedom of speech, right?

Since you're a civilian, I'll go through it with you: most people call it a feather, you know? People see a feather, and they're like, "Feather." But ME, I see things different, that's my *gift*. I see a feather, and I'm just straight up, like, "What if we called this feather the name of some noodle, right? A noodle...in a hat?!" Get real. I just don't see a world where that joke doesn't *destroy*.

It's "PC culture" that's the problem. Let me define "PC culture" for you: "PC culture" is whatever makes me bomb night after night.

The legends couldn't work today. I'm talking, like, the Rockabye Baby Guy, who had that famous gag with the baby falling out of the treetop. Super heady, groundbreaking stuff. Can you imagine him trying that out in front of kids today? They'd be all like, "No. Don't push a baby out of a tree" and "I don't even see what the joke is here" and "Should we really be singing this song to babies?" And when you try to defend yourself, and it's just this complete mob going, "Boo! Get off stage you fucking asshole!" To Rockabye Baby Guy! One of the *greats*.

Look, I'm just saying: you wanna live in a world where the Little Teapot is "height challenged" and "curvy" or fuckin' whatever? Be my fuckin' guest. I'll take short and stout any day. Why? Because having to learn anything new requires admitting that I didn't already know everything in the first place, and that fucking sucks so I won't do it.

These days, half the time, I'm like "... macaroni!" and it's just fucking crickets. One guy in the back coughs. A fuckin' disgrace. So one of two things is true: either I haven't bothered to check in with reality for decades, or it's somehow trans people's fault. And my inability to self-reflect, in combination with an essential moral laziness, means that I'm ve-r-r-r-y fucking inclined to believe it's the latter.

Listen up for a second and learn from one of the greats. Here's a few things that are gold: sitting on a wall and having a great fall. Being a weasel and going "pop!" Calling a feather some kind of pasta. Insulting people with less power than me. Saying "fuck" so much that no one realizes I'm not funny, I'm just mad. Hating my wife, but I have a microphone. Hating women, period, but I have a microphone. Hating myself, but I have a microphone.

Also, a spider that is both itsy and bitsy.

I am *Yankee fucking Doodle*, and I WILL NOT BE CENSORED. ("Being censored" is when I'm less rich than I want to be.) **B**

RIANE KONC (*@theillustrious*) *writes for* **The New Yorker, The New York Times**, *and many other venues. Her new book,* Build Your Own Christmas Movie Romance, *comes out October 2019.*

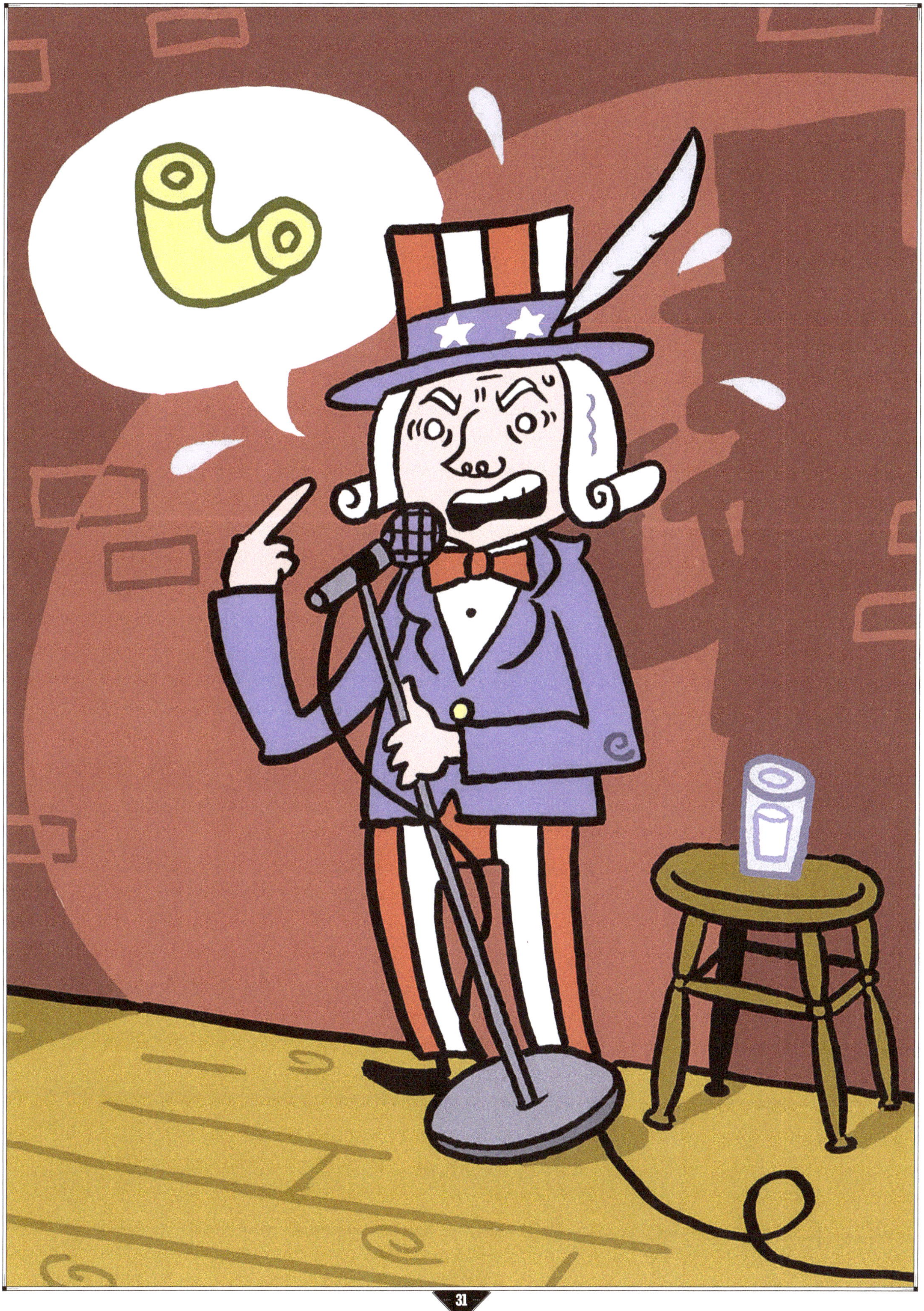

LANCE HANSEN

FADE-OUT

BY DJ DIRTY NEEDLE

THREE SECRET DJ TIPS FOR THE "TWILIGHT OF THE WEST"

Since 2007, DJ Dirty Needle, a.k.a. Mike Tulberski, has been thrilling Brooklyn clubgoers. His monthly party, What The Hell Is This It's Awesome, *just celebrated its tenth anniversary. He also just completed his first year of subscribing to* Foreign Affairs, *the quarterly journal of The Council on Foreign Relations, a prominent non-partisan think-tank.*

Sure, you can build a sweet party playlist for your friends who like the popular stuff on the radio. But what if you want to—or *have* to—impress a group of new friends or co-workers that dig truly underground jams? Well, I hope you enjoy bloodshot eyes, because to even *start* to know this music, you'll be siftin' through Spotify for a straight week. And you can't cut corners, because if you don't ace the mix from the get-go, after a half-hour your guests are gonna bail—leavin' you lookin' at a big, sad display of barely-touched craft beer.

I spin for notoriously picky crowds a lot, and though DJs don't like to give away their secrets, I'm gonna pull back the curtain. Why? Well, to be frank it doesn't seem like that big a deal lately, given the ascent of an increasingly-hardening dogmatism across the political spectrum within Western democracies that's led to an ominous de-valuing of freedom of expression, making these traditionally tolerant countries appear confused, even fragile.

So sit back and chillax—let's get to buildin' a killer vibe!

SUPER-SECRET DJ TIP #1:

Crowds into underground tunes gotta be impressed immediately when they arrive. To them, music is more than a pleasant background distraction—it's a pheromone-like giveaway of your personal style, and it tells them you're cool enough to like. But never fear, my friend. Frontload your playlist with Iggy Pop's '70s stuff, any Beastie Boys from *Paul's Boutique* to *Hello Nasty*, and a few pre-reunion LCD Soundsystem singles, and you're well on your way to making sure everyone at your bash will be stickin' around.

Yet, even with a successful start to your playlist, a dark part of me can't help but want your guests to leave early. I want them to realize, after being at the party for only a little while, that no playlist, or amount of drinks, or even the possibility of sexual intercourse can distract them from a gnawing unease over the unprecedented divide between the left and the right in the most stalwart democracies…a divide that has citizens seeing those on the opposing side not as fellow countrymen, but hostile foreigners bent on their personal destruction.

Of course, that degree of overwhelming angst will not happen at your party, or at any party, unfortunately. Or, I mean, fortunately. Sorry. Anyway, just forget it—it's all good.

SUPER-SECRET DJ TIP #2:

When your guests have sauntered 'round your soirée for about an hour, it's time to make 'em put on their boogie shoes. At this point in the playlist, have ready a moderately-known-but-not-killed-by-a-million-commercials James Brown tune. Then, hit 'em with "Tainted Love"—I don't mean the '80s New Wave version by Soft Cell, I'm talkin' the raw but obscure Northern Soul original, done by Gloria Jones in 1964. They won't have heard the tune done like this before, and since it's such a sick banger, they'll be movin' furniture to make a bigger dance floor.

Having a party in which the jams are off the hook, however, now comes with a terrible price. Is not each night, each hour, *each banger* another opportunity lost? Is a smoky, sweaty, red-hot club the most conducive environment for an awakening to the current cultural and generational shifts tearing at the seams of nations that have, for so long, been models of stability and openness? Probably not. And who, I ask you, ensures that these opportunities for greater awareness are denied, again and again? Me, that's who—because I'm a good DJ. In our current political reality, I'm the fabled pied piper, my seductive music leading crowds blissfully to the little death of continued civic indifference.

I could lessen the damage. I could switch my night to a totally lame Monday, but oh, no—Your Highness couldn't give up his Saturday set. So I recklessly keep the most possible people groovin', like a guy who knows he's too drunk to drive yet still gets behind the wheel, simply for the sybaritic thrill of it. Actually, I wish my dangerous behavior was fueled by alcohol; I think then I could control it. But I'm motivated by something more potent: *skillz*. And a passion for my craft that lies so deep within that it may be impossible to extirpate. You said it, my friends—this DJ is *sick*.

SEAN LAFLEUR *(@handle) has written satire for* **The Onion**, *actual journalism for newspapers in D.C. and Los Angeles areas, and currently writes down song requests on napkins as a DJ in New York City.*

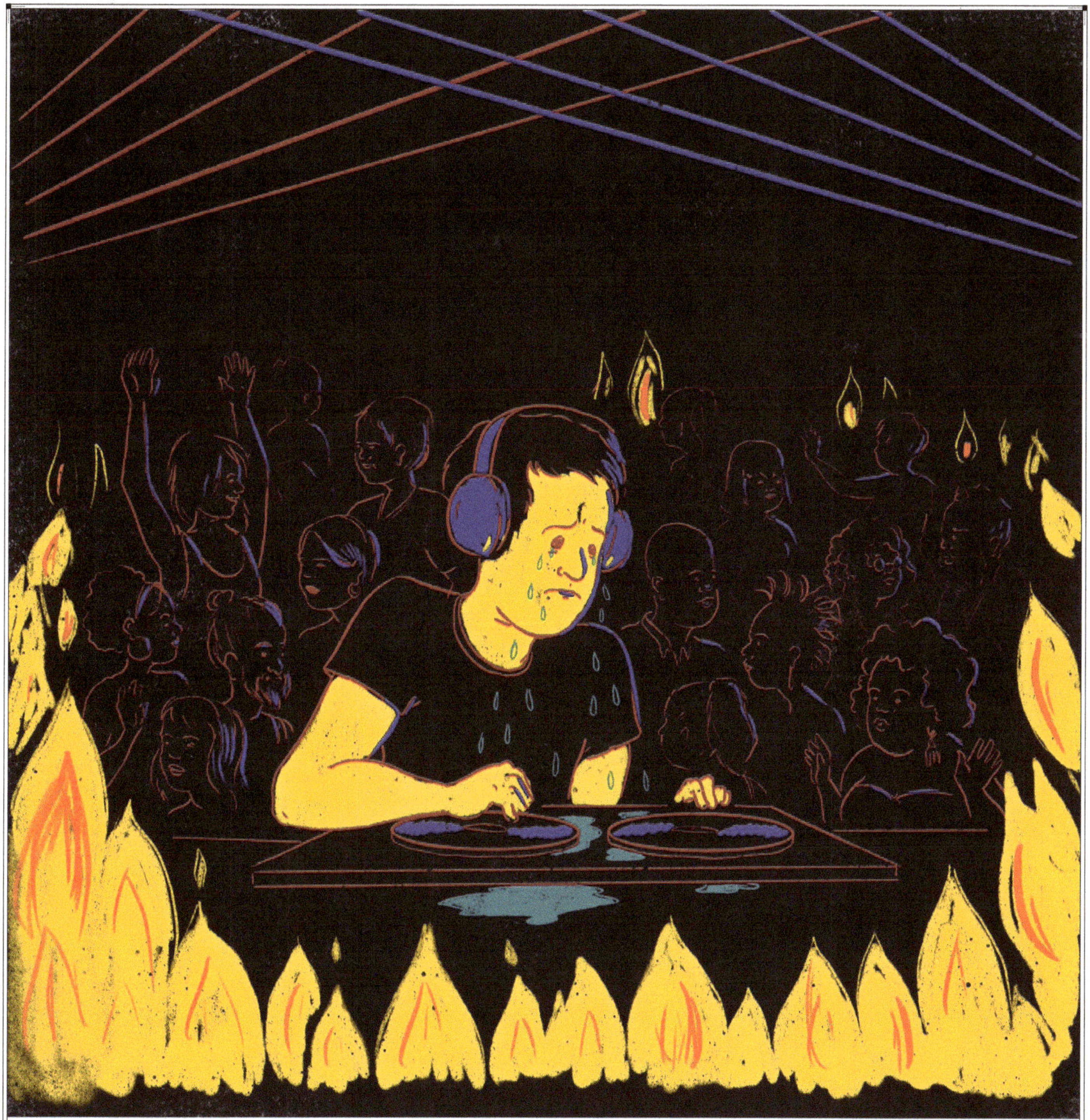

EMILY FLAKE

SUPER-SECRET DJ TIP #3:

Once they've been shakin' it for about a solid 45, the crowd will start to trust you…time to take 'em somewhere. Fussy crowds dig an exotic international detour; they can feel worldly, but also get a little *sex-ay*. Latin, French or Indian tunes are excitingly foreign, but most will recognize the rhythms. Think of it as takin' the crowd to the deep end of the pool…but still givin' 'em a life preserver.

With each set I play, I am being torn apart. Sure, I look perfectly at ease, one hand setting the vinyl spinning free while the other floats just above the mixer, fingers effortlessly finding their exact place on the knobs and buttons. But inside, I am in agony—caught between love and duty, style and substance, self and nation. As long as Western democracy remains in its current troubled condition, I will always be locked in the maddening, isolated center between these opposite poles, as if the cross-fader knob on my mixer has become frozen in the middle. Two songs playing at once…but the beat never matches, the transition never completes.

It is an untenable existence. If this torture becomes unbearable, I will be left with the most extreme choice: I will have to leave this world behind—this little, constricting, pleasure-bound paradise—and go. Go out and do something, *anything*.

Maybe voter-outreach volunteer work? At least on the weekdays, when I'm rarely booked. B

BY EMMA BREWER

WANTED: HIGH-CONFLICT, PARANOID BABY BOOMER TO RUN ESSENTIAL DEPARTMENT

We want you to join our ranks as a Director of Operations, reporting to the CEO. The hours would be 11:00 am to around 3:00 pm (give or take), Monday through Friday. Work from home most Fridays, each time it rains, or when your college-aged daughter has cramps. Your team will be happy to pick up the slack.

Responsibilities will include: Printing every email you receive (including the attachments) and leaving them in heaps by the communal printer; wandering to and fro with a plastic container of salad; and issuing brutal, cutting remarks to your assistants. You'll spend roughly thirty percent of each day buying and printing Groupons that you may or may not use.

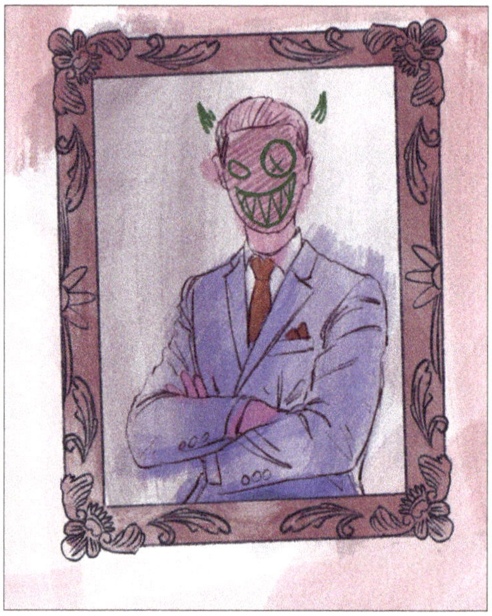
MARQUES DUGGANS

Once every week or so, we'll expect you to call your assistant Peter in a breathless panic, demanding he drop everything to sort through which email print-outs you have taken care of (none), and which Groupon print-outs have expired (nearly all). While he's at it, he can look for the Post-It where you scribbled all your passwords. No, not that one, Peter. The new one.

The bulk of each work day will be spent hunkered in your office with your second assistant Ana, recounting for her, stream-of-consciousness style, every thought that passes through your head. Topics will include: that time you were late to a Billy Joel concert; a rude thing your daughter's dentist said to you in 2003; all the reasons Paul Ryan will be a great President one day. It's important to deliver each monologue without blinking or breaking eye-contact, so that your underling learns the vital skill of murmuring in agreement for hours, an idiot's grin aching on her face. Pivot suddenly, near the end, to blast her with a withering and baseless accusation about her job performance. Ideally, your staff will leave each encounter confused, exhausted, and a tiny bit unhinged—just like you!

Lunchtimes will be spent at your leisure, hovering by Ana's desk for ninety minutes describing every salad you've ever eaten, while Ana nods brightly, a cup of chicken pot pie cooling into a miserable gel by her side. Once you begin to settle in, make your team even more on edge by muttering sly homophobic jokes to Ana when Peter isn't around, and sly anti-immigrant theories to Peter when Ana isn't around. With any luck, each member of your staff will feel a rush of pure, shuddering nausea whenever they hear the seal-bark of a smoker's laugh that precipitates your approach.

Relevant Experience Required: At least twenty years in the industry, or long enough to have developed bitter enemies within our vendor companies, competitors, and in-house. Regale Ana with tales of how Maura in the Tribeca office used to steal your best ideas, and how she is possibly bugging your desk even now. Before he leaves, ask that moron Peter where the fax machine is, so he can lead you to the scanner for the ninth time.

Technical Skills: must be able to call IT several times a day, in increasingly belligerent tones. Your subordinates will handle everything else relating to Excel, Microsoft Office, Adobe, and the four internal systems needed to run daily operations.

Length of Contract: Despite a blossoming file in HR with your name on it, you can expect to linger for decades, traumatizing generations of assistants, until you retire with a modest cheese party. At that point, we look forward to clearing away four hundred cracker packets from Hale and Hearty, and nearly a thousand expired Groupons.

Salary: 265,000 (negotiable). **B**

EMMA BREWER *(@emargaretbrewer) contributes to* McSweeney's, Weekly Humorist, Jellyfish Review, *and elsewhere. She's working on a short story collection; find more at emmamargaretbrewer.com.*

The Funniest Two Books
Since the Old and New Testament

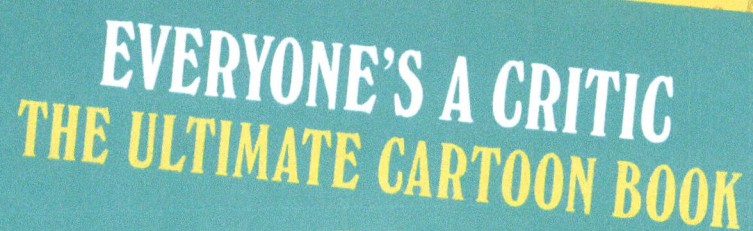

Princeton Architectural Press

www.papress.com

NEW FROM SIMON RICH

"One of the funniest writers in America."
—NPR

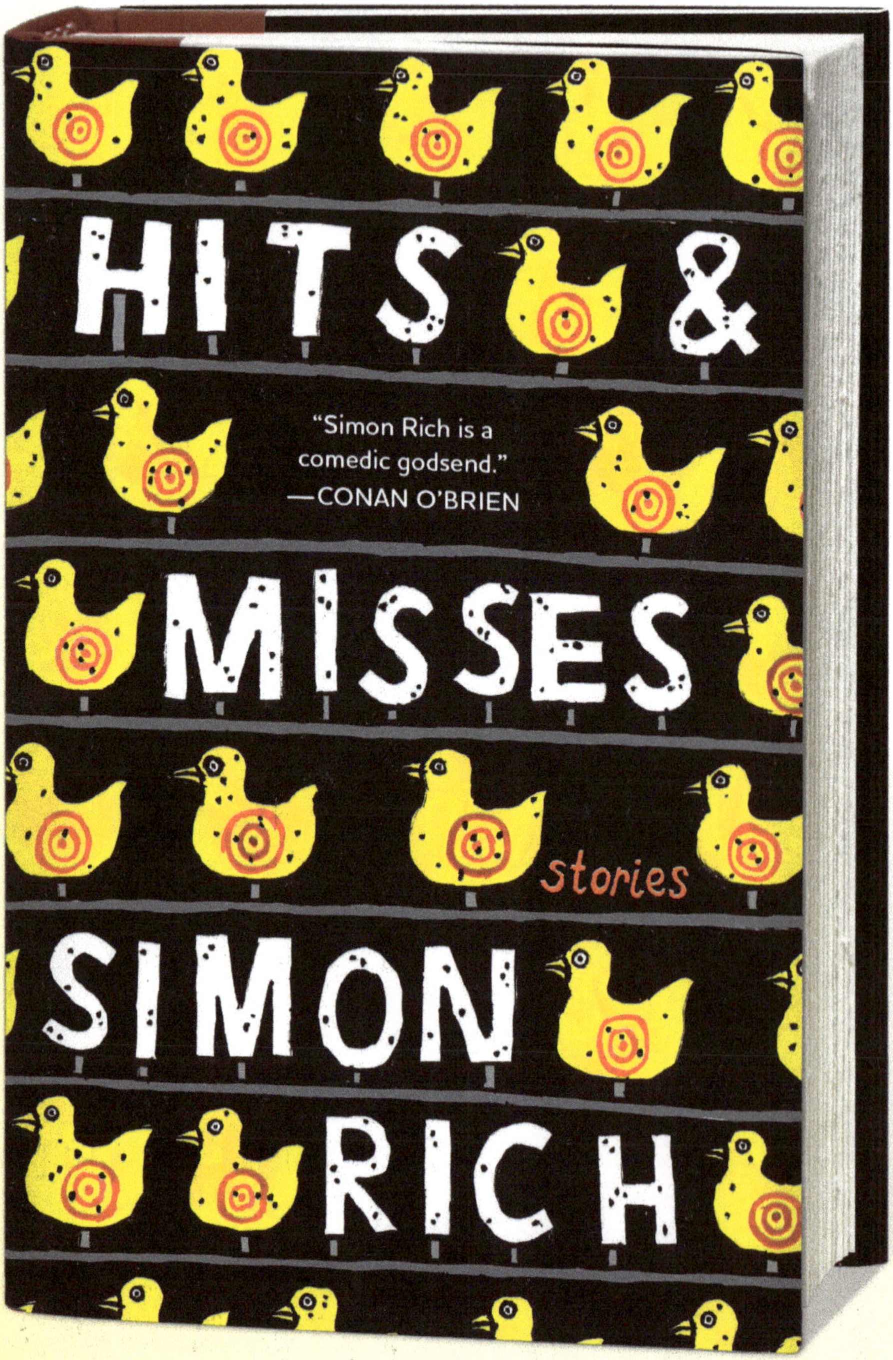

"A motherlode of silly, inventive, absurd brilliance."
—CONAN O'BRIEN

"First-rate comedy with a heartbeat.... One of my favorite authors."
—B.J. NOVAK

"The Stephen King of comedy writing.... HITS AND MISSES is his best collection of stories."
—JOHN MULANEY

ON SALE NOW
in hardcover, ebook, and audio
littlebrown.com

LITTLE, BROWN AND COMPANY
Hachette Book Group

Inky Fingers!

To me, art has always seemed like a kind of magic, and so I approach artists, even the friendly ones, with a mixture of respect, wonder and more than a little apprehension. It's impossible to watch a network of shaky, uncertain-seeming lines suddenly snap into a version of reality without suspecting that The Devil surely had a hand in it. Of course as Jonathan Plotkin shows us below, it's sweat, not Satan, that's responsible…but I'm not taking any chances. Consider this special section a burnt offering.—MG

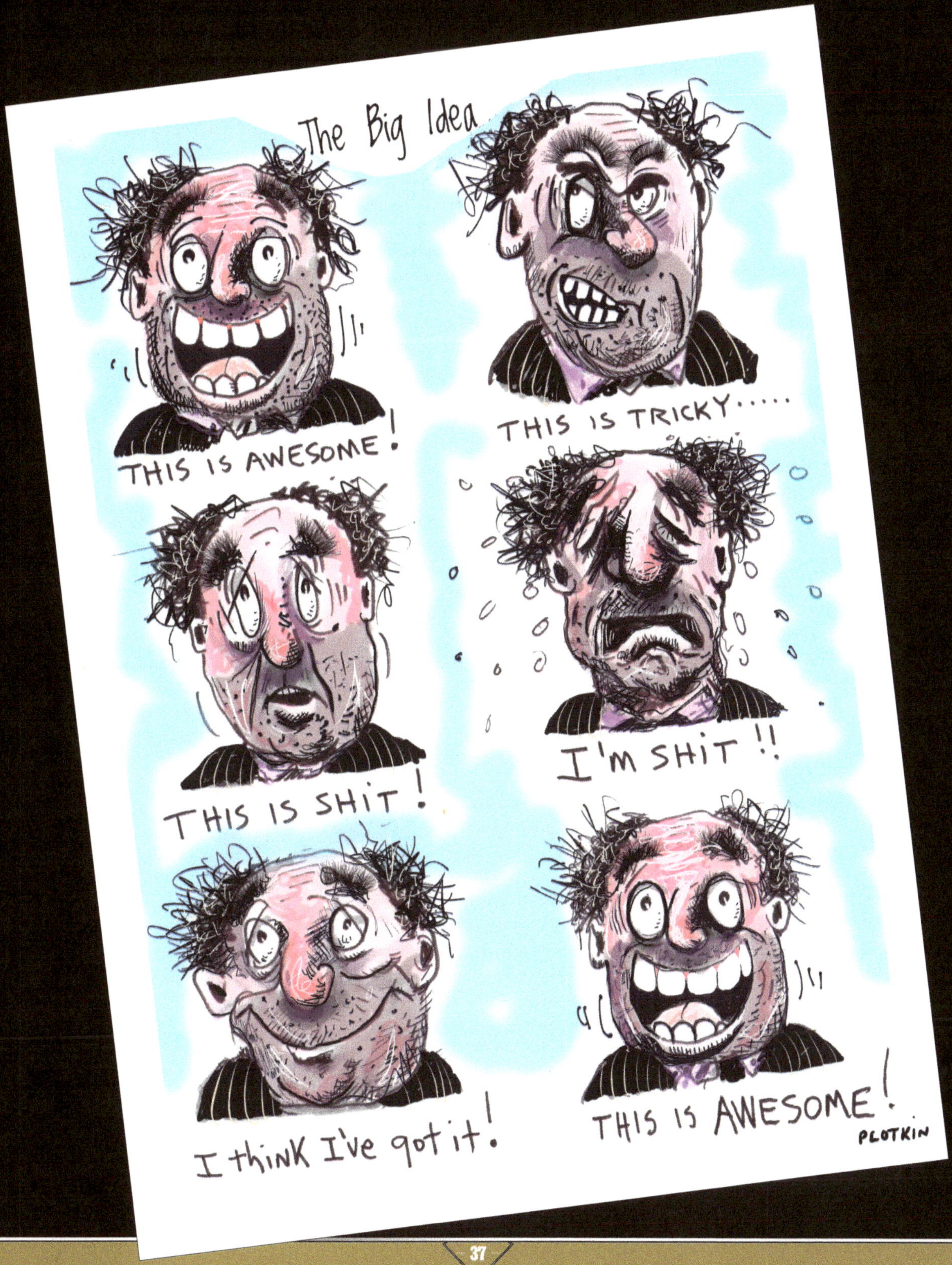

The Big Idea...
THIS IS AWESOME!
THIS IS TRICKY.....
THIS IS SHIT!
I'M SHIT!!
I think I've got it!
THIS IS AWESOME!
PLOTKIN

My Comedy Albums

"Early in my career, I recorded a stack of comedy and novelty LPs, to varying degrees of success. Here are just a handful of old favorites."

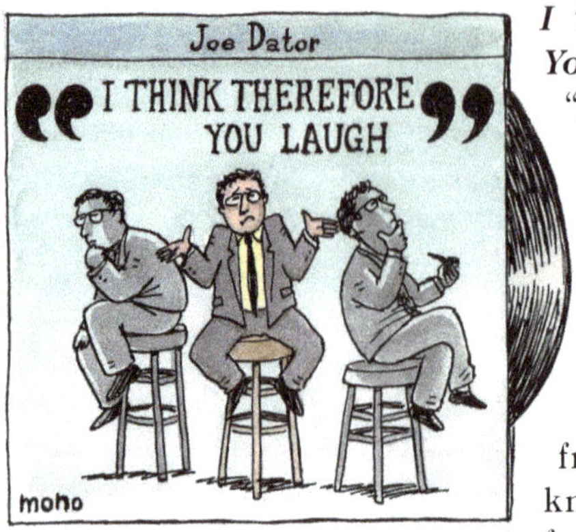
Joe Dator
" I THINK THEREFORE YOU LAUGH "

I Think Therefore You Laugh **(1961)**
"My first album. The record company sold me as an intellectual comic like Mort Sahl or Shelley Berman, even though all my material came from a book of knock-knock jokes for preschoolers."

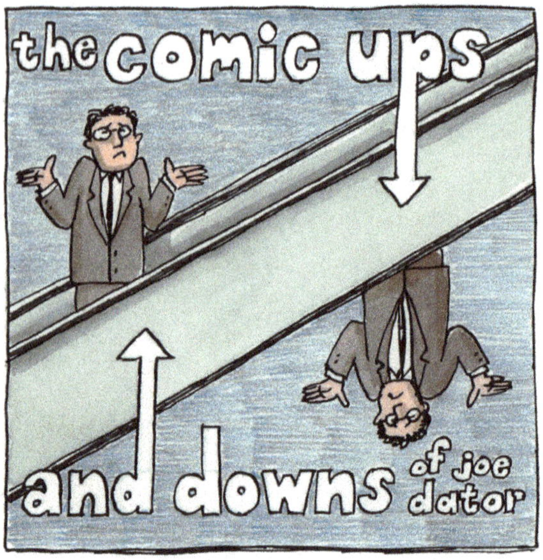
the comic ups
and downs of joe dator

The Comic Ups And Downs of Jae Dator **(1962)**
"Back then, comics did send-ups of whatever crazy new technology was out there. I did an album of material about escalators, which I thought were just a passing fad."

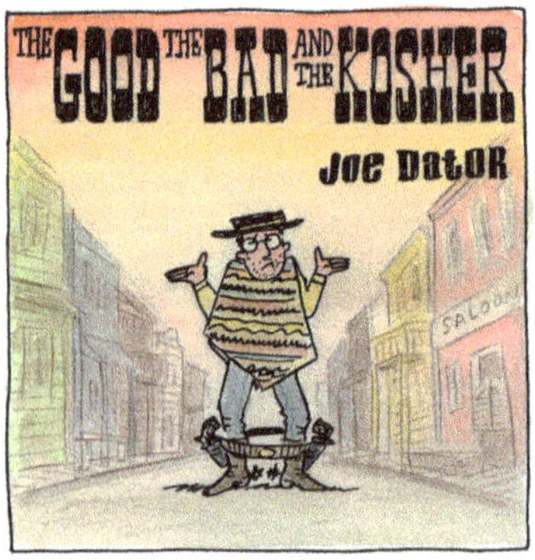
THE GOOD THE BAD AND THE KOSHER
JOE DATOR
SALOON

The Good The Bad and The Kosher **(1964)**
"The Clint Eastwood westerns were a big hit at the time, but this was an album of material about my Jewish upbringing. It was criticized for being hackneyed, and for the fact that I am not Jewish."

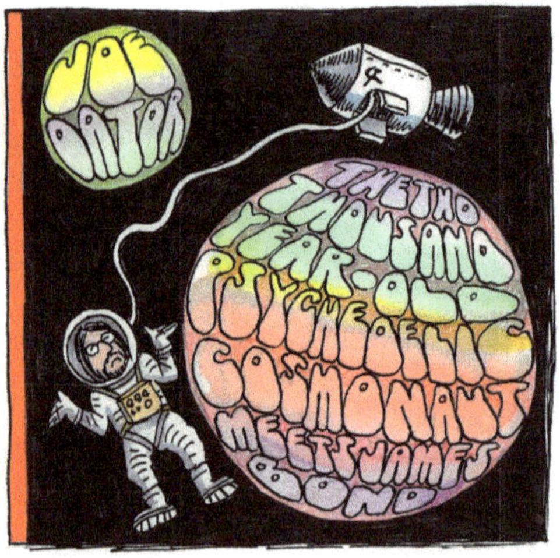
JOE DATOR
THE TWO THOUSAND YEAR-OLD PSYCHEDELIC COSMONAUT MEETS JAMES BOND

The 2000-Year-Old Psychedelic Cosmonaut Meets James Bond **(1968)**
"I can't really say very much about this album. I have no memory of recording it."

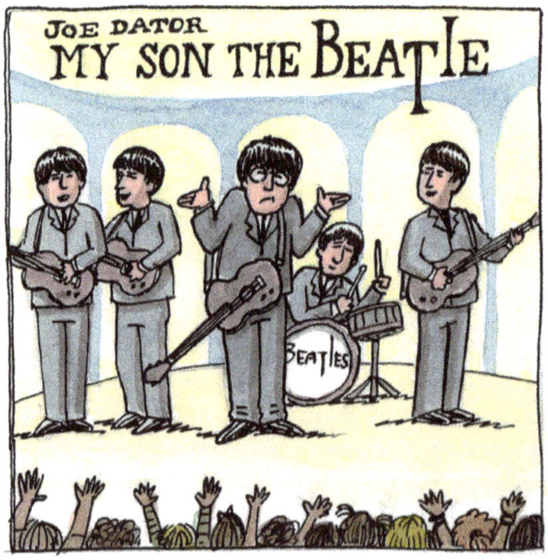
JOE DATOR
MY SON THE BEATLE
BEATLES

My Son The Beatle **(1966)**
"This was my attempt at a quickie Beatlemania cash-in. The record company hated it and refused to release it, which is a shame because I'd actually convinced John, Paul, George and Ringo to write 12 original songs and record them with me. Oh well."

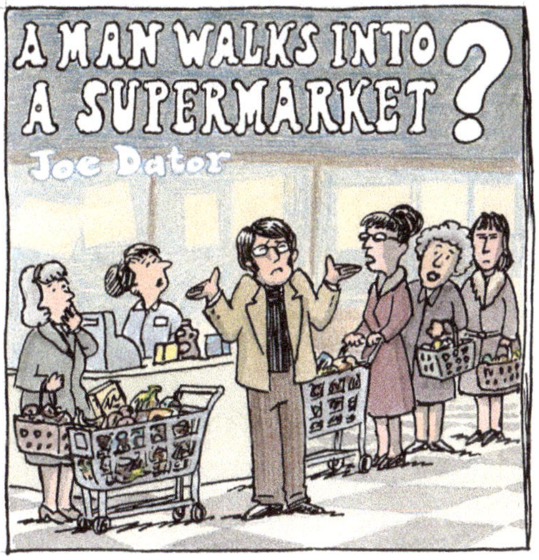
A MAN WALKS INTO A SUPERMARKET?
Joe Dator

A Man Walks Into A Supermarket? (1970)
"I tried to send up Women's Lib by doing jokes about how crazy it would be if a man had to do the grocery shopping. A&P put up the money for the album, so after every joke I had to say something about their specials, which threw my timing off a little."

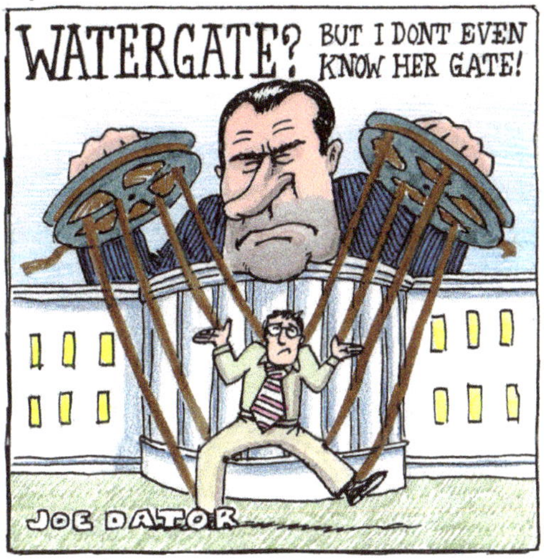
WATERGATE?
BUT I DONT EVEN KNOW HER GATE!
JOE DATOR

Watergate? But I Don't Even Know Her Gate! (1974)
"I jumped on the Watergate bandwagon just like everyone else. My material was mostly favorable to Nixon, but in my defense I wasn't really up on current events."

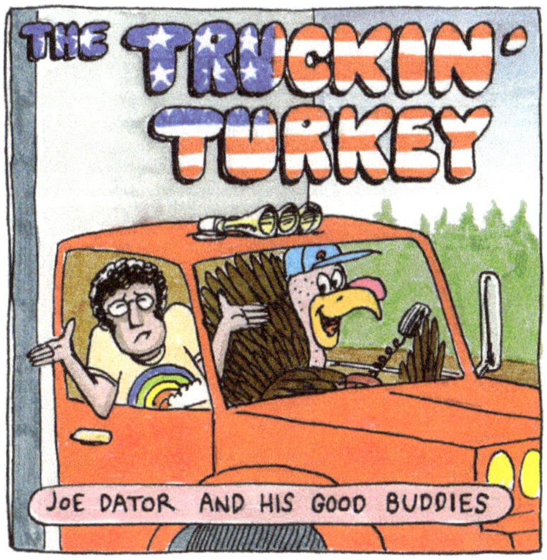
THE TRUCKIN' TURKEY
JOE DATOR AND HIS GOOD BUDDIES

The Truckin' Turkey (1976)
"On this one I did parodies of the most popular trucking songs of the latter half of 1976, all 150 of them."

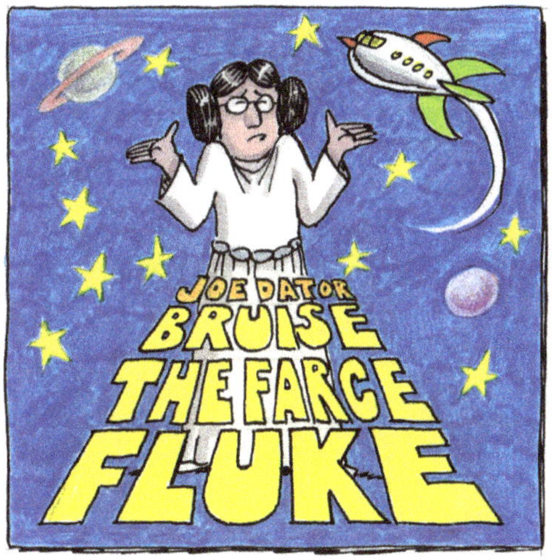
JOE DATOR
BRUISE THE FARCE FLUKE

Bruise The Farce Fluke (1978)
"This was recorded live at Carnegie Hall, during the brief period when it was converted into a roller disco."

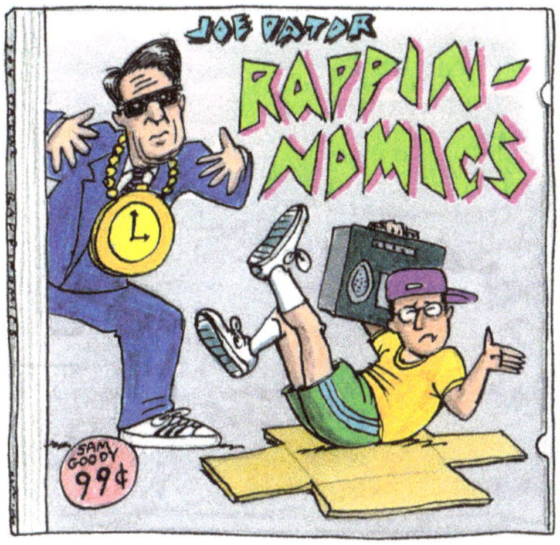
JOE DATOR
RAPPIN-NOMICS
SAM GOODY 99¢

Rappin-Nomics (1984)
"All I can say about this is that there are some things in life you're going to be proud you did, and some you'll wish you hadn't done…I could not be more proud of this album."

"Sadly, all of these are long out-of-print, but if you're lucky you can still find one or two at swap meets and used record shops. The sleeves may be faded, but the jokes are as timeless as the 12" plastic discs they're printed on." B

JEREMY NGUYEN

"Honestly, same."

"My Logan is already hiding from shooters at a fourth grade level."

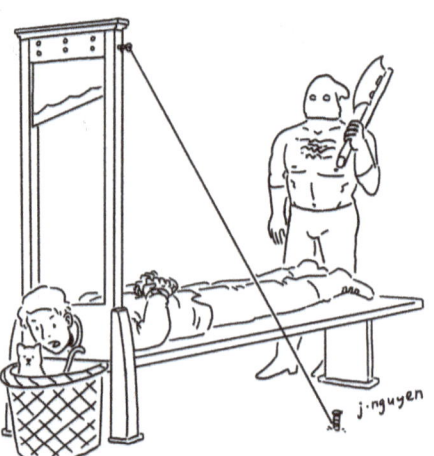

"Sadie, get out of there!"

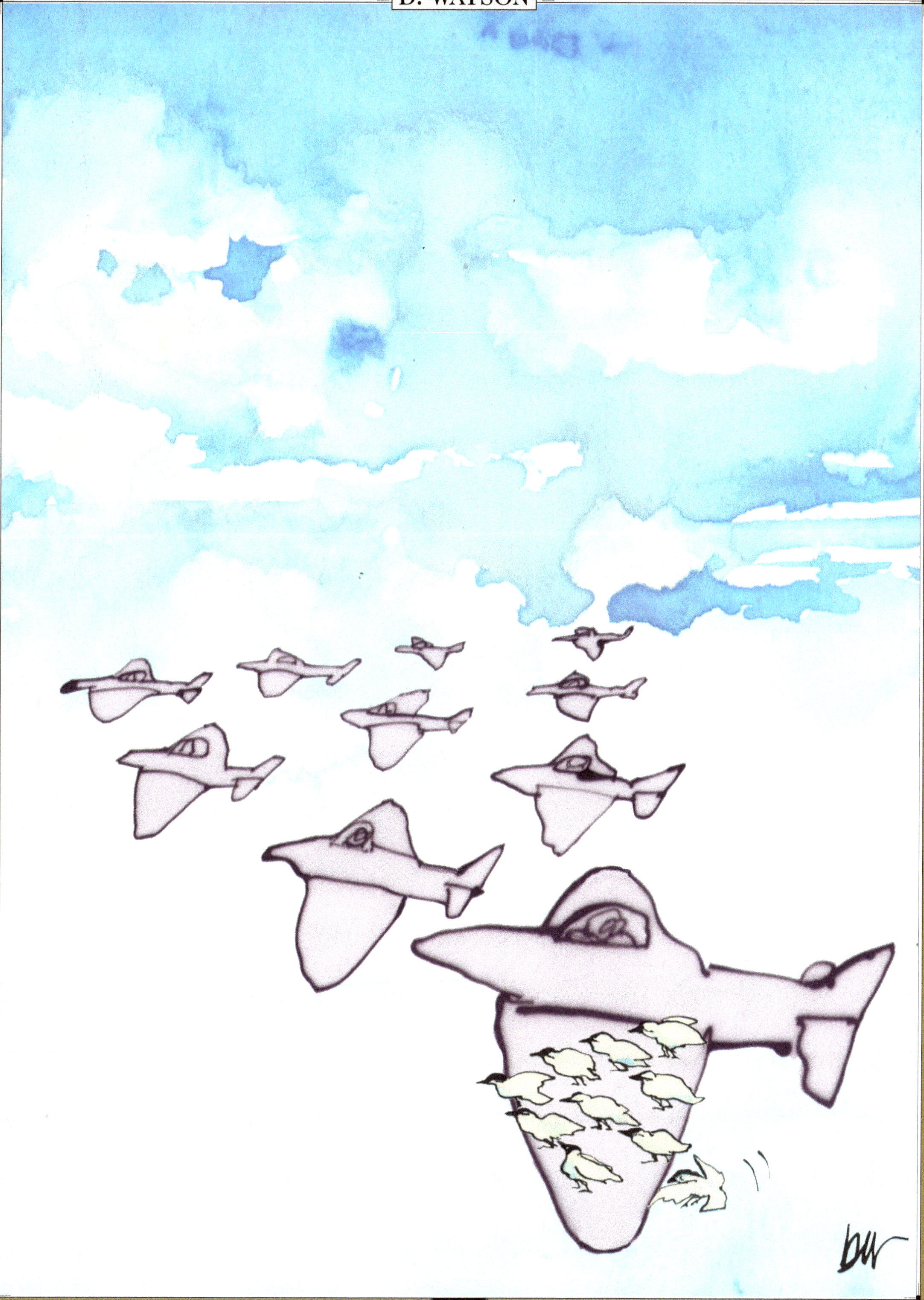

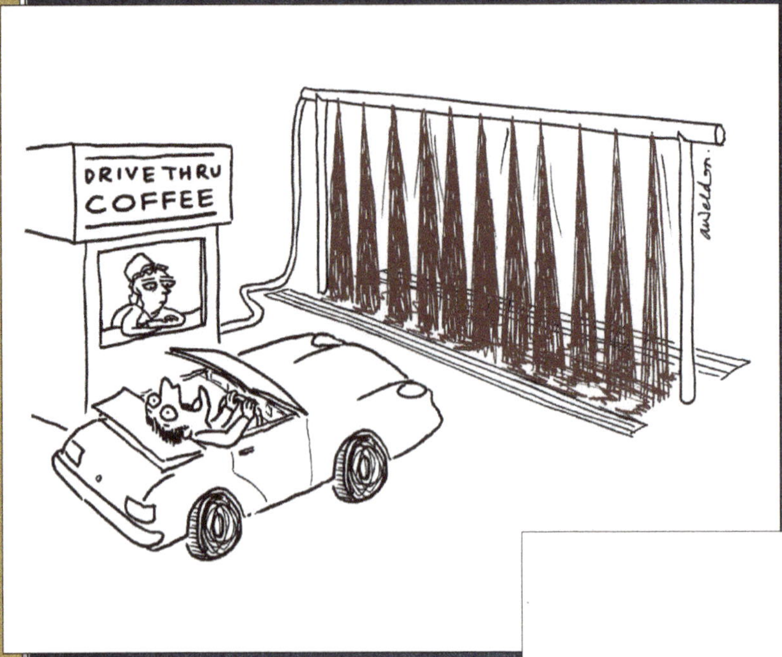
DRIVE THRU
COFFEE

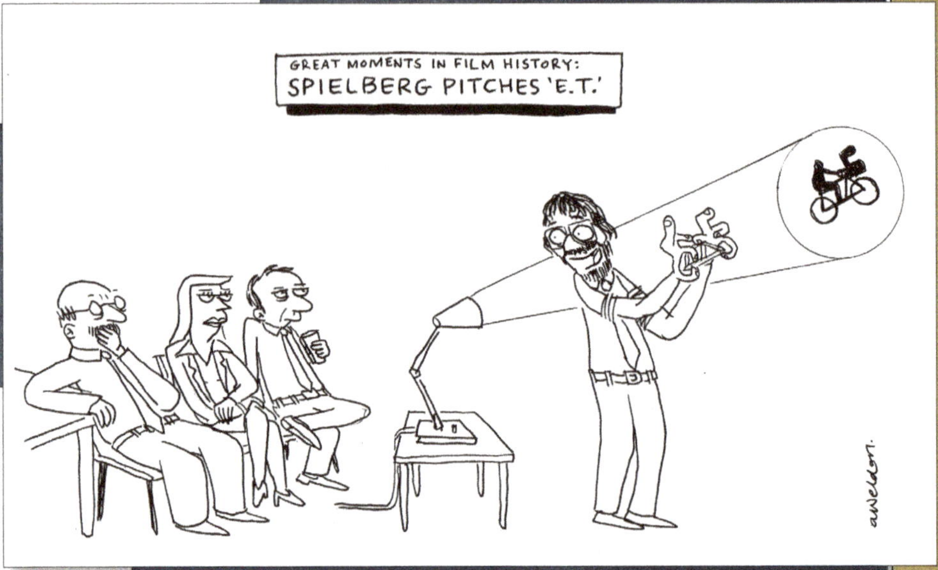
GREAT MOMENTS IN FILM HISTORY:
SPIELBERG PITCHES 'E.T.'

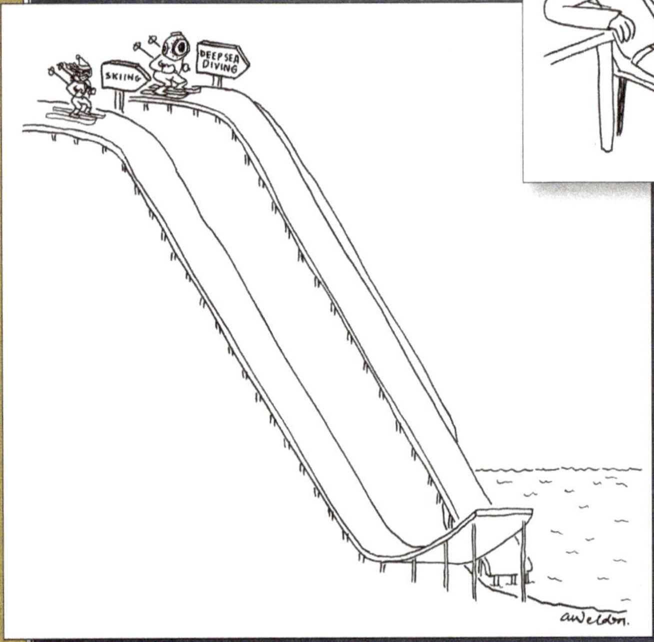
SKIING
DEEP SEA DIVING

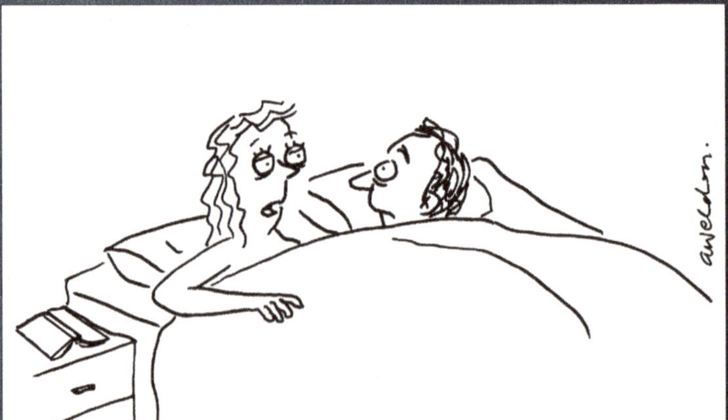

"COULD YOU NOT?
I'M LEAVING THAT
EROGENOUS ZONE FALLOW."

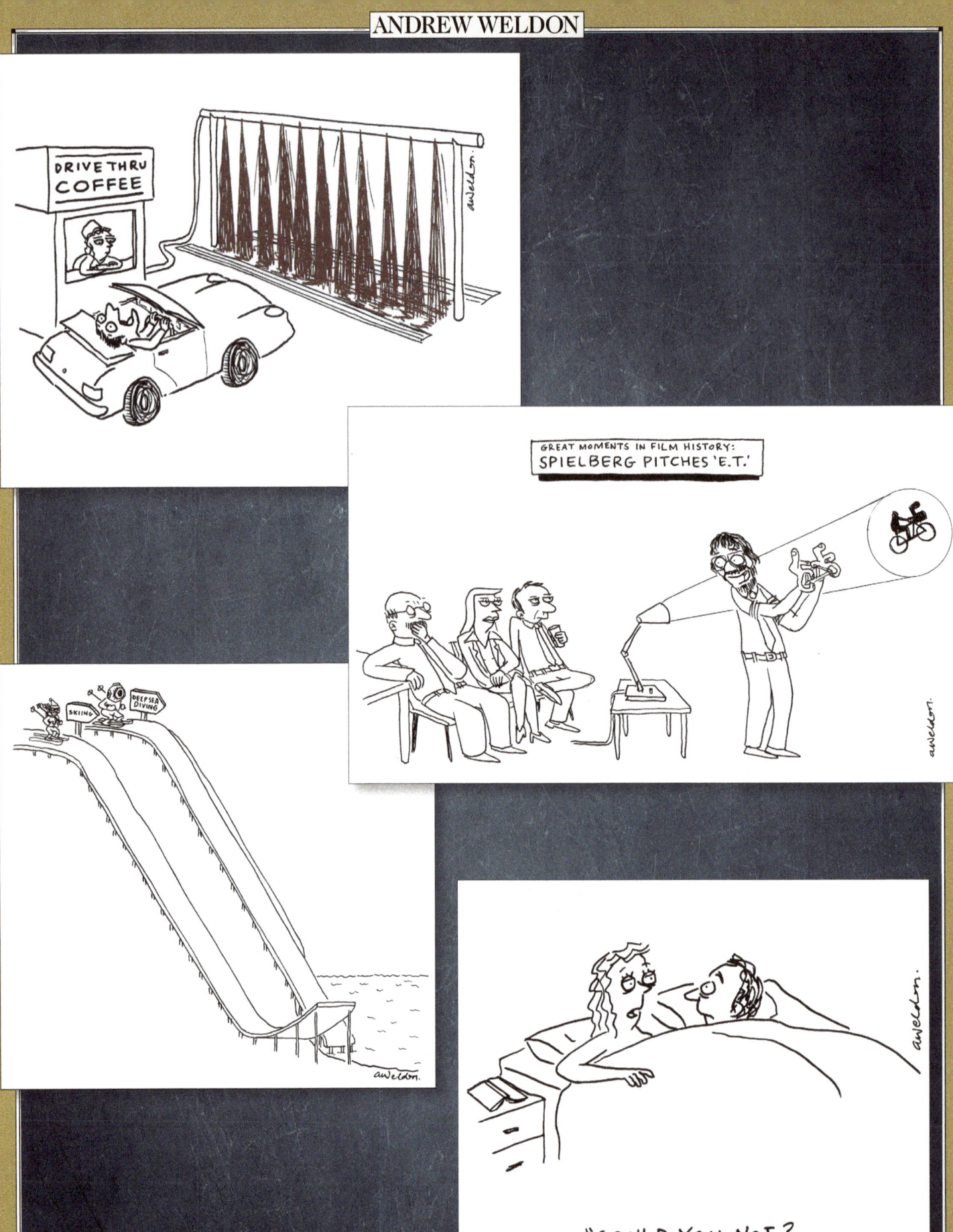

To the Rescue...

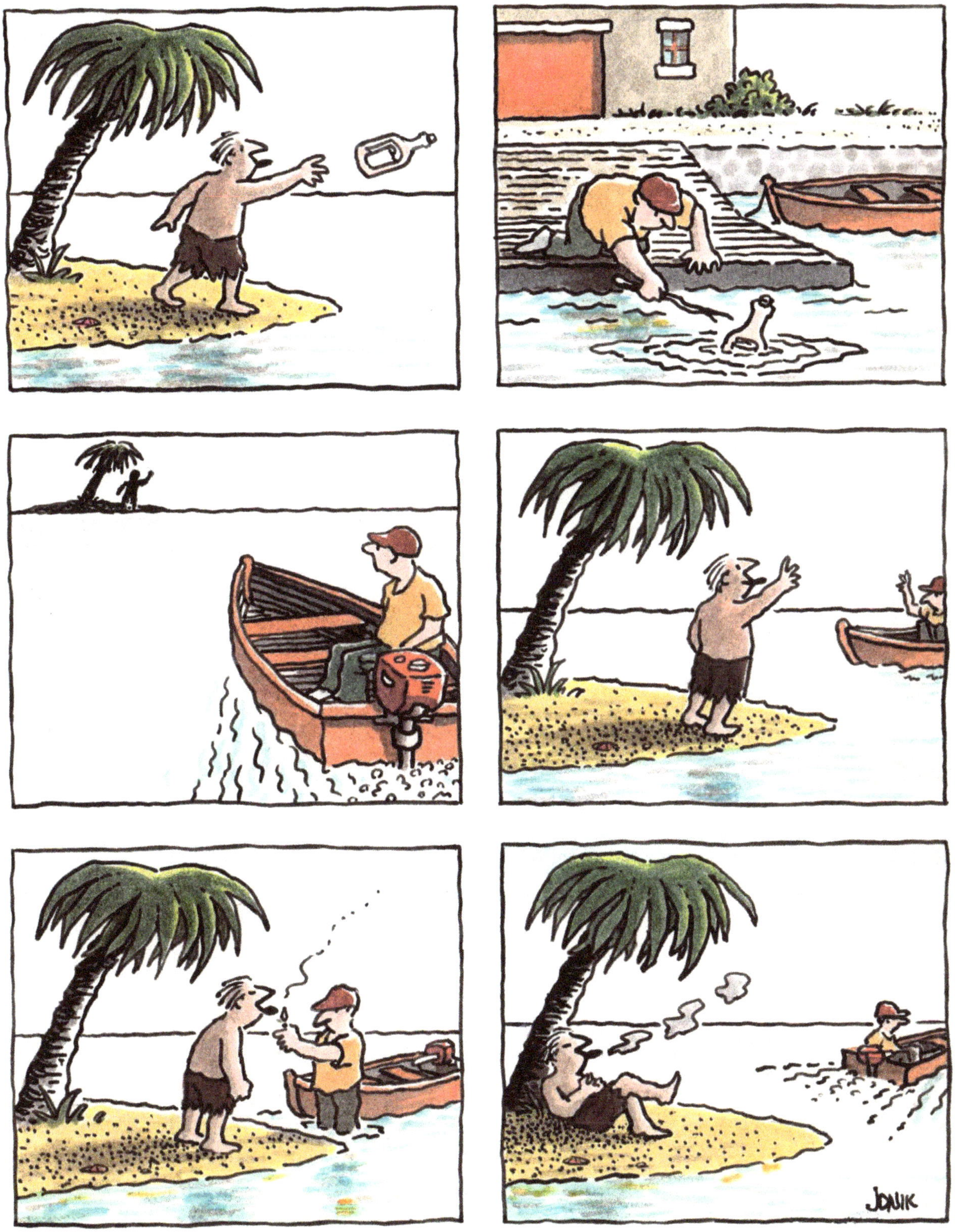
JONIK

B

One Day In the Park

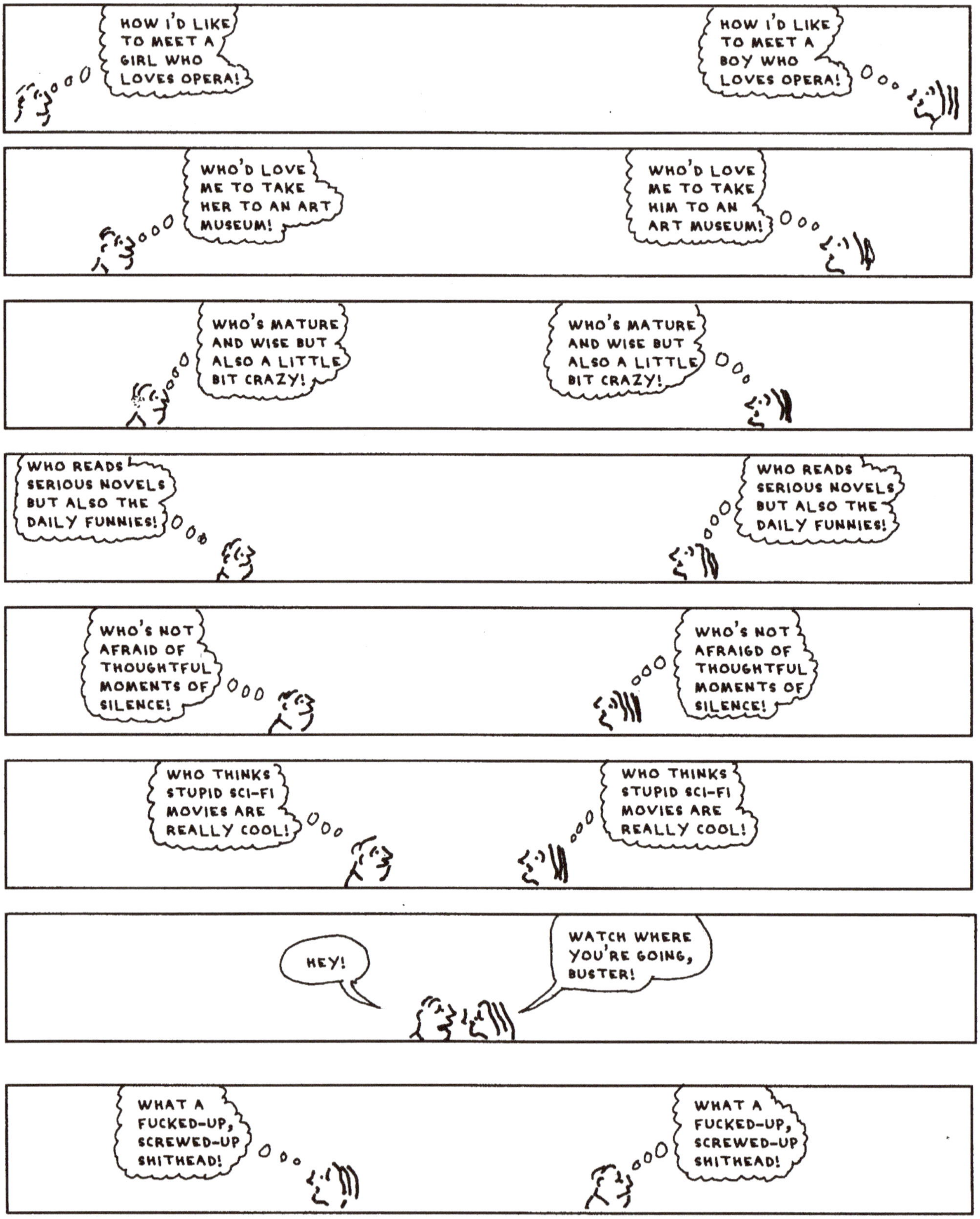
HOW I'D LIKE TO MEET A GIRL WHO LOVES OPERA!
HOW I'D LIKE TO MEET A BOY WHO LOVES OPERA!
WHO'D LOVE ME TO TAKE HER TO AN ART MUSEUM!
WHO'D LOVE ME TO TAKE HIM TO AN ART MUSEUM!
WHO'S MATURE AND WISE BUT ALSO A LITTLE BIT CRAZY!
WHO'S MATURE AND WISE BUT ALSO A LITTLE BIT CRAZY!
WHO READS SERIOUS NOVELS BUT ALSO THE DAILY FUNNIES!
WHO READS SERIOUS NOVELS BUT ALSO THE DAILY FUNNIES!
WHO'S NOT AFRAID OF THOUGHTFUL MOMENTS OF SILENCE!
WHO'S NOT AFRAIGD OF THOUGHTFUL MOMENTS OF SILENCE!
WHO THINKS STUPID SCI-FI MOVIES ARE REALLY COOL!
WHO THINKS STUPID SCI-FI MOVIES ARE REALLY COOL!
HEY!
WATCH WHERE YOU'RE GOING, BUSTER!
WHAT A FUCKED-UP, SCREWED-UP SHITHEAD!
WHAT A FUCKED-UP, SCREWED-UP SHITHEAD!

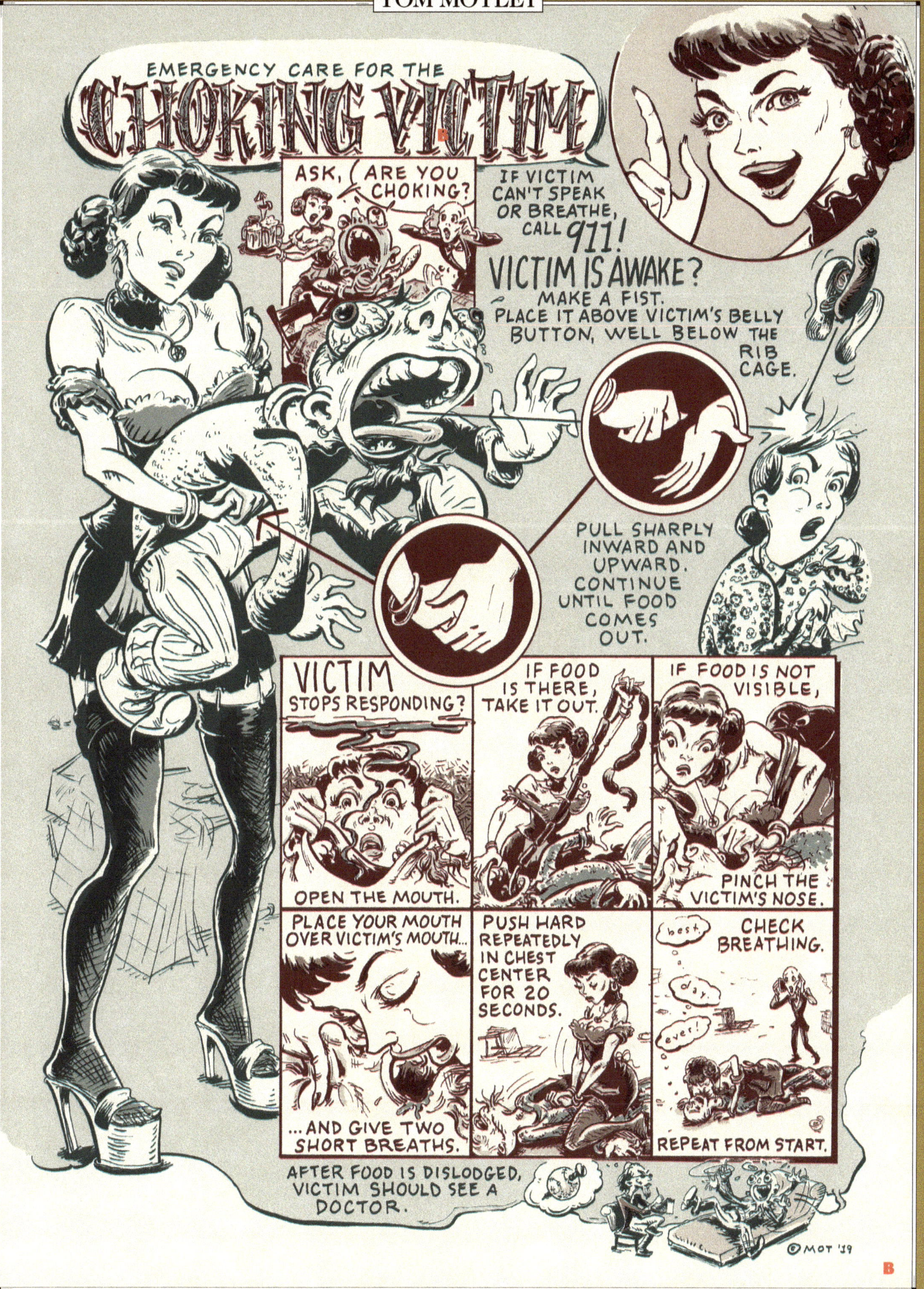
EMERGENCY CARE FOR THE
CHOKING VICTIM
ASK, ARE YOU CHOKING?
IF VICTIM CAN'T SPEAK OR BREATHE, CALL 911!
VICTIM IS AWAKE?
MAKE A FIST.
PLACE IT ABOVE VICTIM'S BELLY BUTTON, WELL BELOW THE RIB CAGE.
PULL SHARPLY INWARD AND UPWARD. CONTINUE UNTIL FOOD COMES OUT.
VICTIM STOPS RESPONDING?
OPEN THE MOUTH.
IF FOOD IS THERE, TAKE IT OUT.
IF FOOD IS NOT VISIBLE,
PINCH THE VICTIM'S NOSE.
PLACE YOUR MOUTH OVER VICTIM'S MOUTH...
...AND GIVE TWO SHORT BREATHS.
PUSH HARD REPEATEDLY IN CHEST CENTER FOR 20 SECONDS.
CHECK BREATHING.
best.
day.
ever!
REPEAT FROM START.
AFTER FOOD IS DISLODGED, VICTIM SHOULD SEE A DOCTOR.
© MOT '19

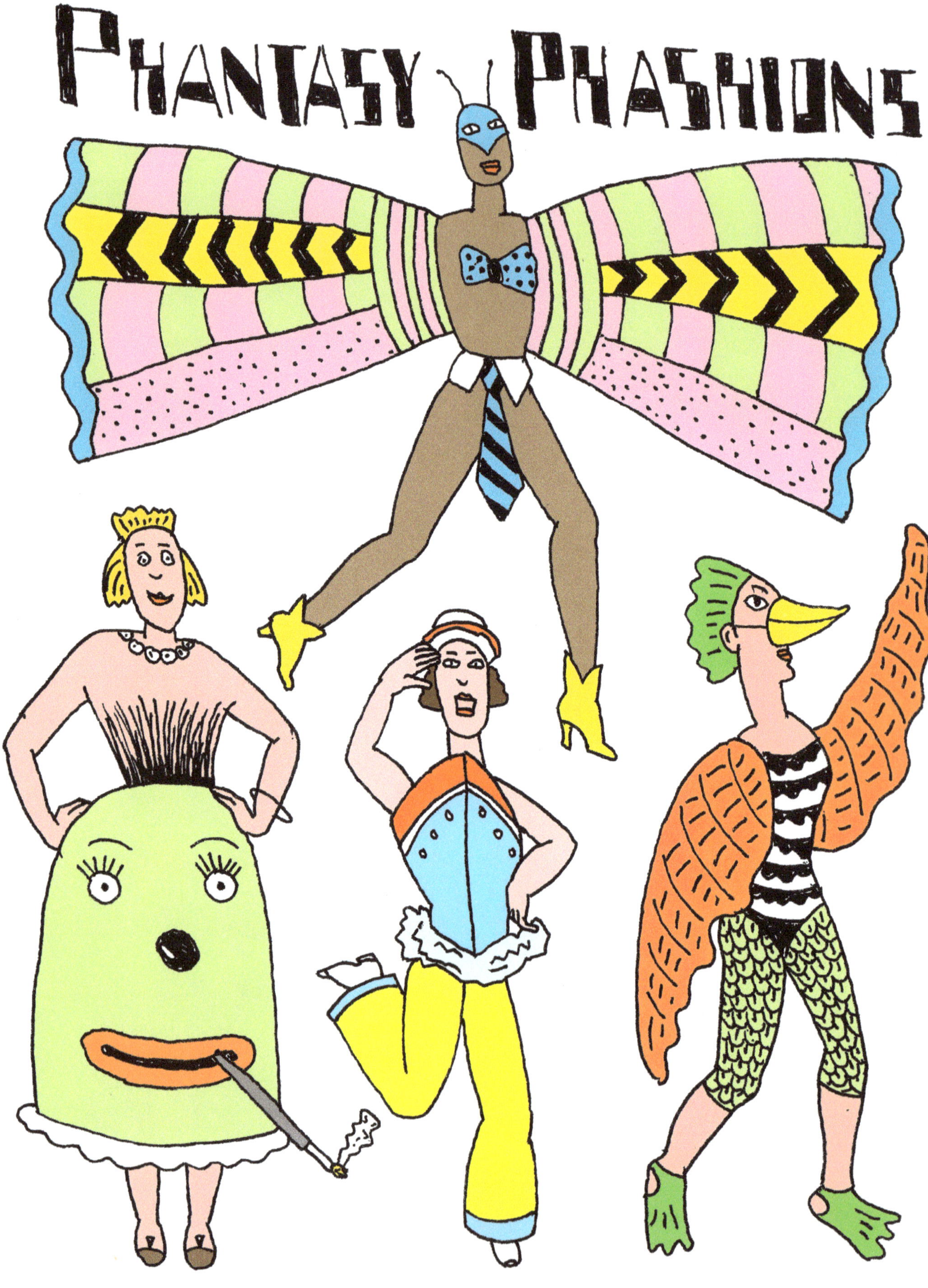
PHANTASY PHASHIONS

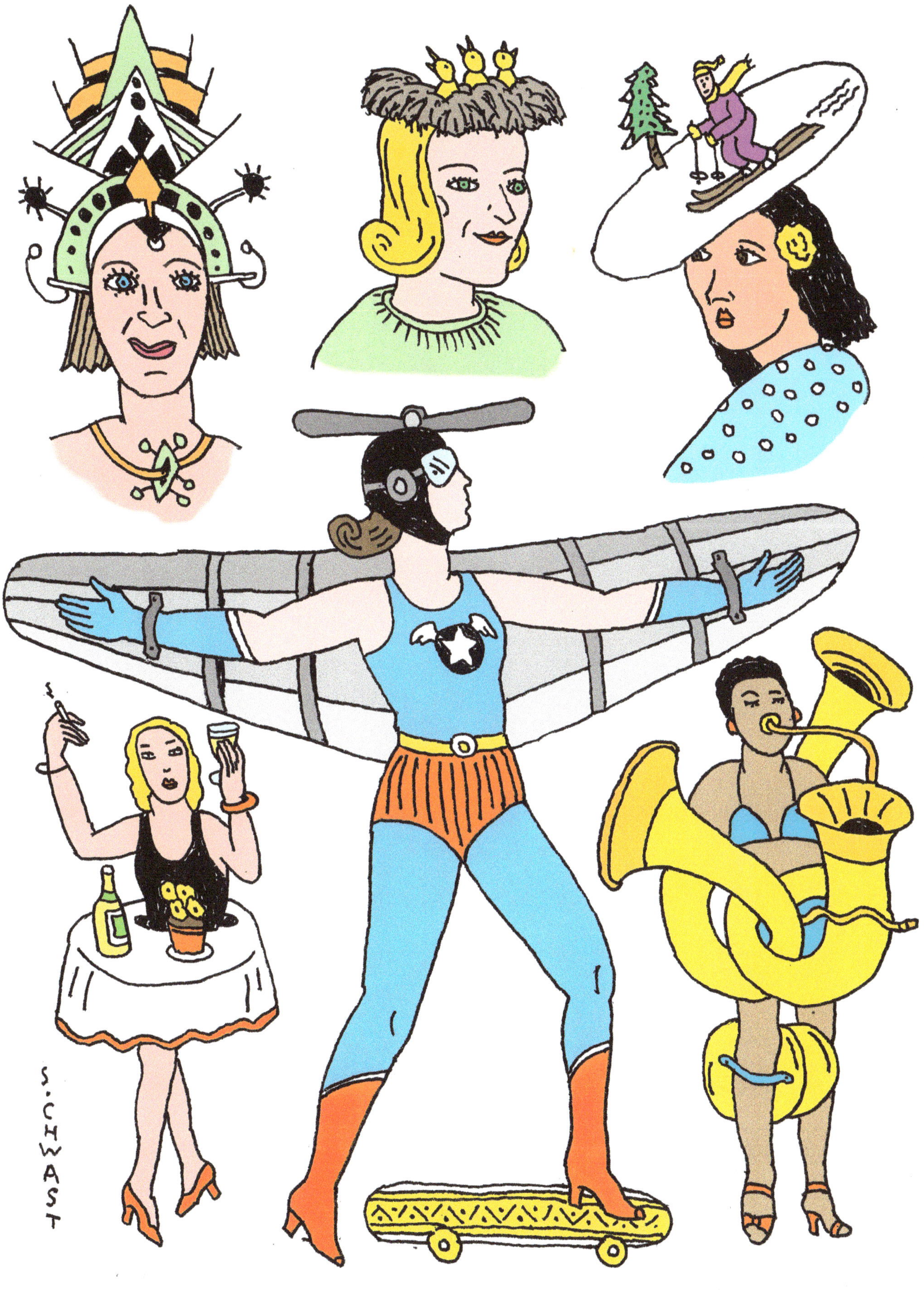
S. CHWAST

Welcome to the Shit Show

MARK BRYAN

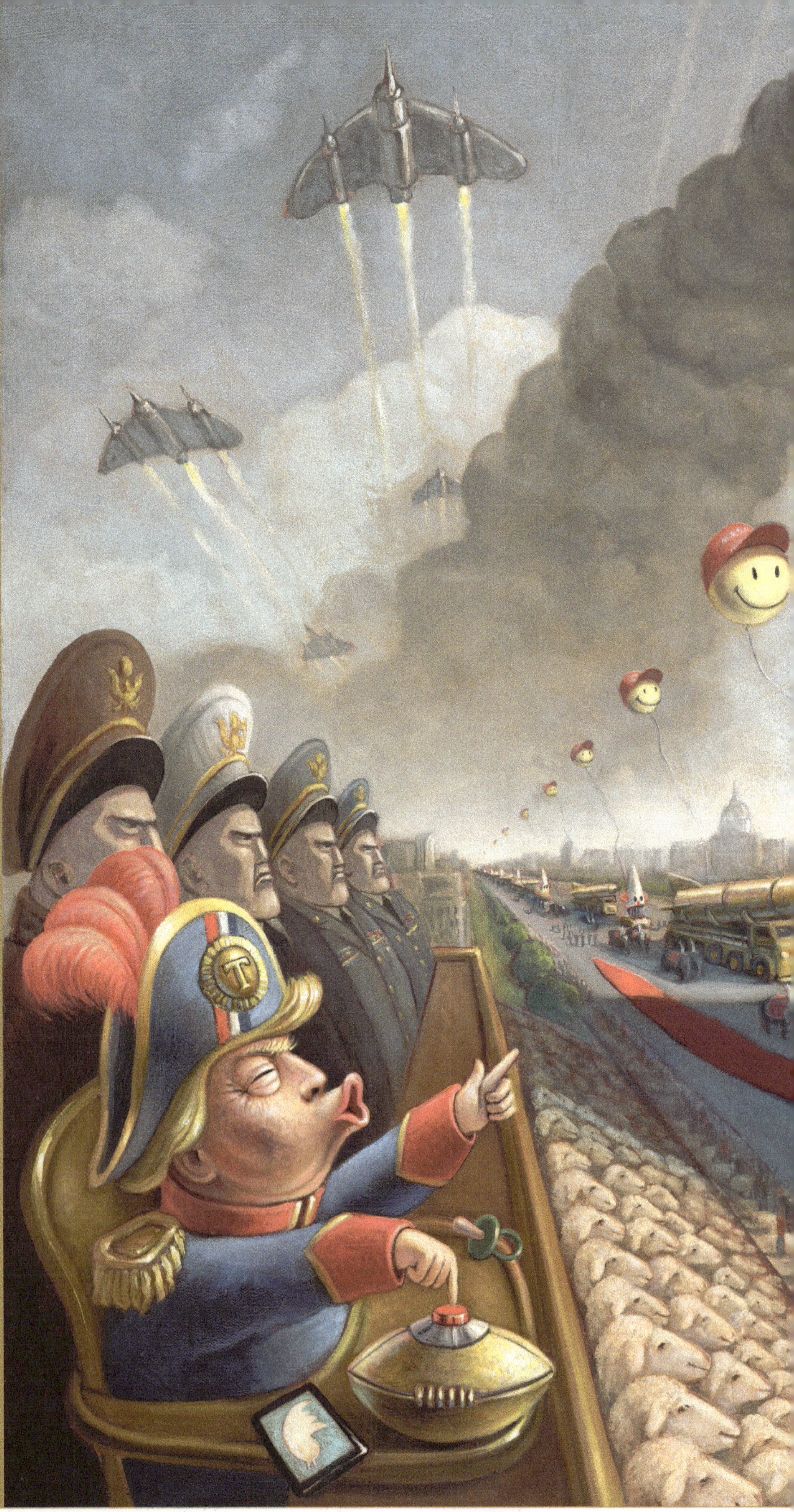

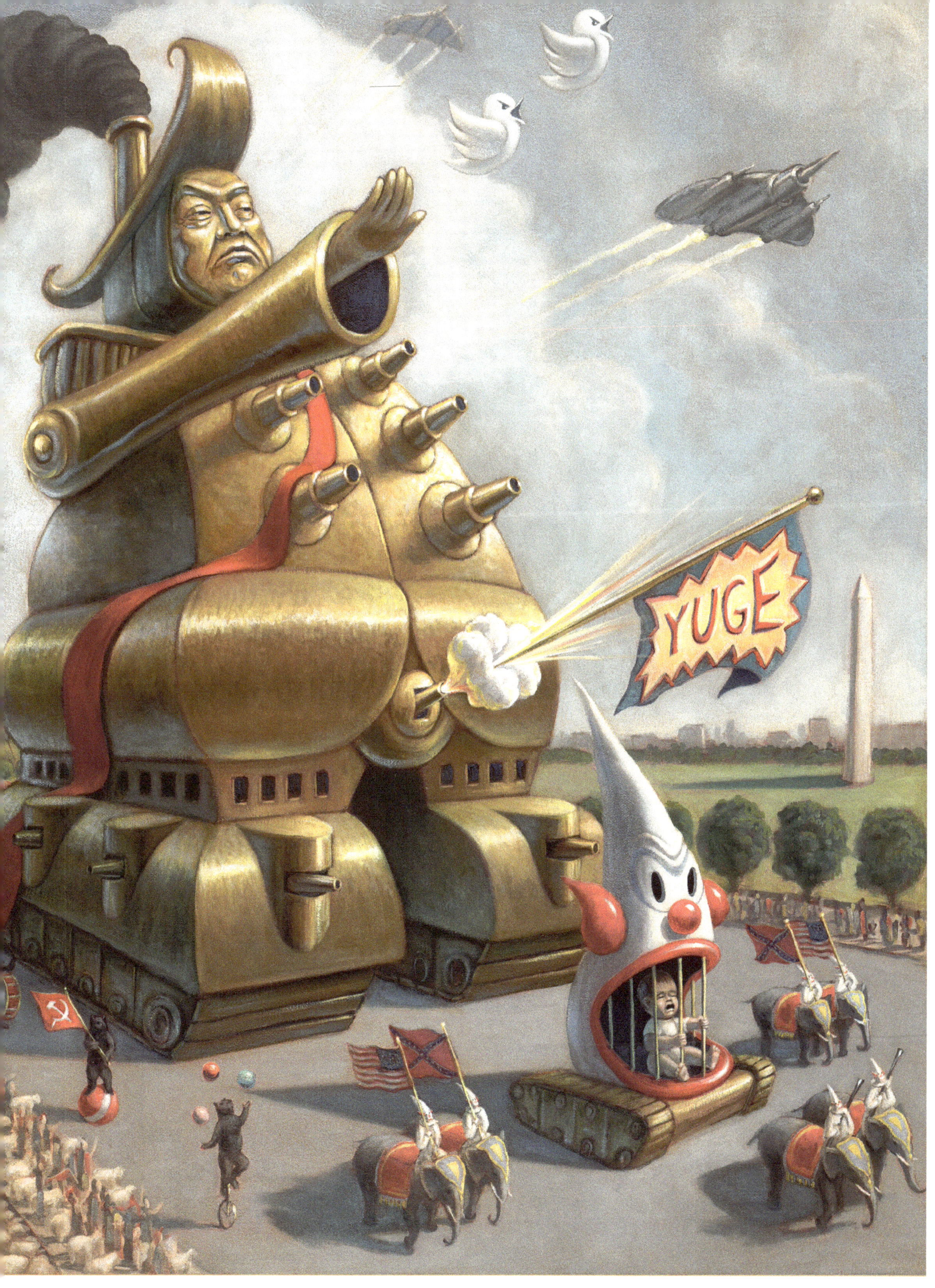
YUGE

PAUL KLEBA

KLEBA

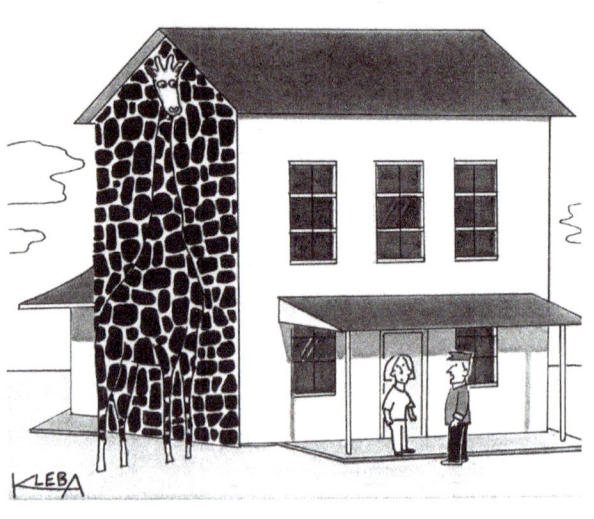

"Well if you do see her, let us know."

KLEBA

HUSTLER
PENTHOUSE
PLAYBOY
KLEBA

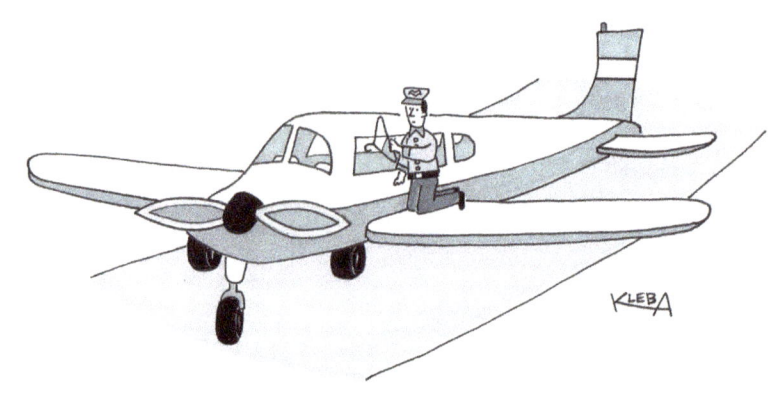

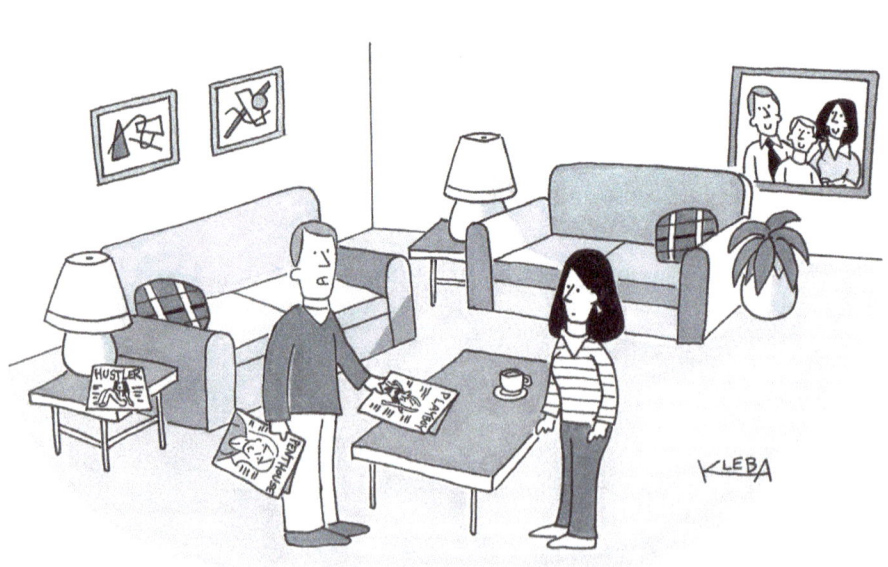

"If I lay enough of these around, maybe he'll stay off the internet."

LANCE HANSEN

Marty Grosz is an American jazz rhythm guitarist, banjoist, composer and vocalist. Marty agreed to talk with me about his life, and the life and work of his father, German Expressionist artist and social critic, George Grosz. These strips are based on those conversations.

An Interview With Marty Grosz

"I was born in Berlin"

1930... Came over in '33.

The '20s and early '30s were a time of conflict and stress in Germany.

There was a lot of street fighting... a lot of rioting.

The Fascists were fighting the Communists.

Most of the German authorities, it seems, favored the fascists.

These gangs of thugs would march around and beat each other up.

And law enforcement would kind of look the other way.

Though not so much when it was the left wing guys.

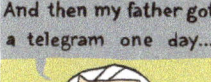
And then my father got a telegram one day...

Berlin

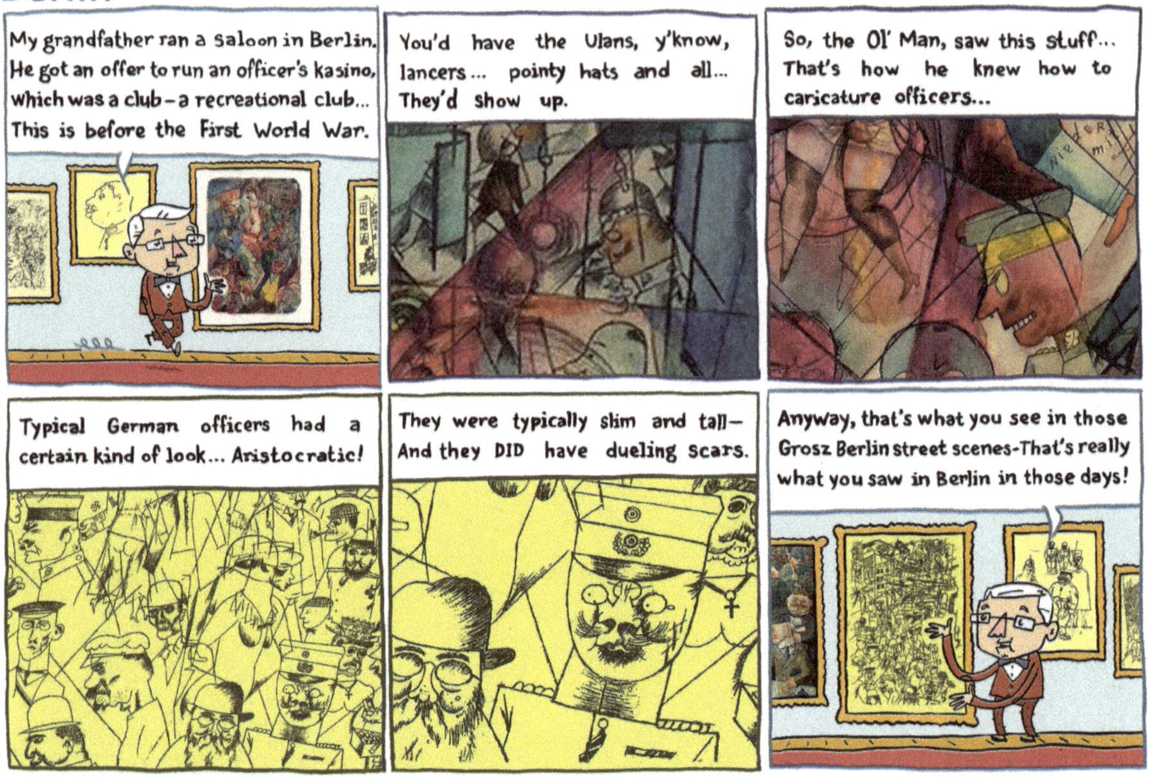
My grandfather ran a saloon in Berlin. He got an offer to run an officer's kasino, which was a club–a recreational club... This is before the First World War.
You'd have the Ulans, y'know, lancers... pointy hats and all... They'd show up.
So, the Ol' Man, saw this stuff... That's how he knew how to caricature officers...
Typical German officers had a certain kind of look... Aristocratic!
They were typically slim and tall– And they DID have dueling scars.
Anyway, that's what you see in those Grosz Berlin street scenes-That's really what you saw in Berlin in those days!

"He was tried three times..."

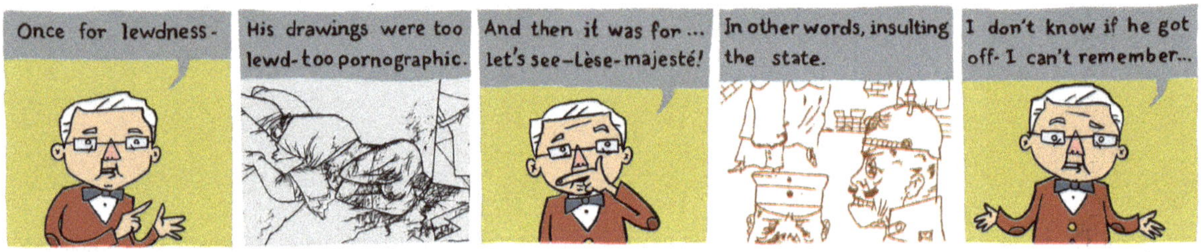
Once for lewdness-
His drawings were too lewd-too pornographic.
And then it was for... let's see–Lèse-majesté!
In other words, insulting the state.
I don't know if he got off- I can't remember...

A Close Call

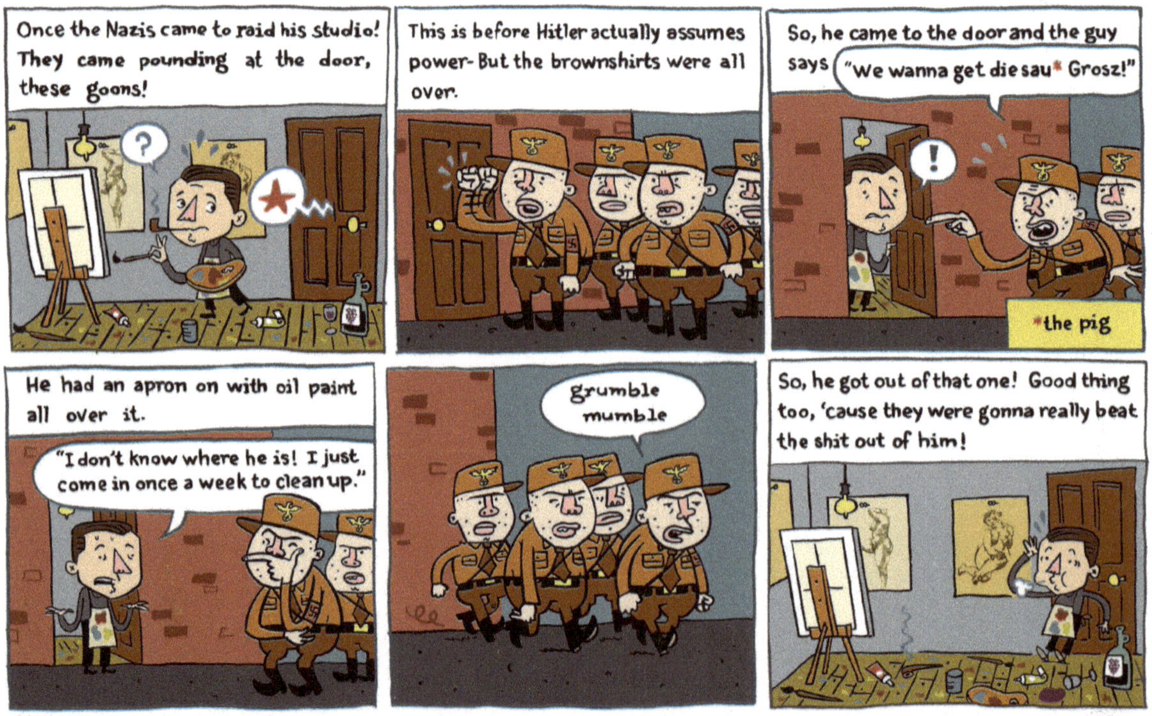
Once the Nazis came to raid his studio! They came pounding at the door, these goons!
This is before Hitler actually assumes power- But the brownshirts were all over.
So, he came to the door and the guy says
"We wanna get die sau* Grosz!"
*the pig
He had an apron on with oil paint all over it.
"I don't know where he is! I just come in once a week to clean up."
grumble mumble
So, he got out of that one! Good thing too, 'cause they were gonna really beat the shit out of him!

Centerpiece

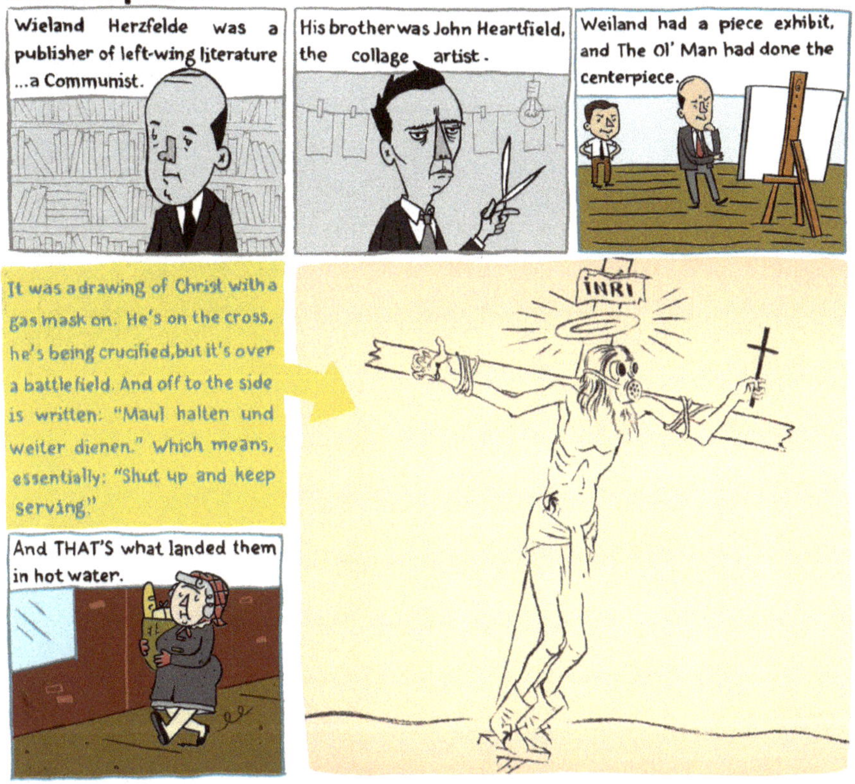
Wieland Herzfelde was a publisher of left-wing literature ...a Communist.
His brother was John Heartfield, the collage artist.
Weiland had a piece exhibit, and The Ol' Man had done the centerpiece.
It was a drawing of Christ with a gas mask on. He's on the cross, he's being crucified, but it's over a battlefield. And off to the side is written: "Maul halten und weiter dienen." Which means, essentially: "Shut up and keep serving."
INRI
And THAT'S what landed them in hot water.

A Complaint

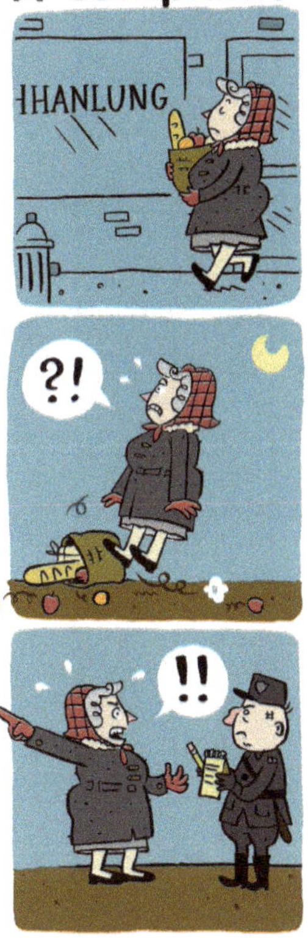
IHANLUNG
?!
!!

The Third Trial

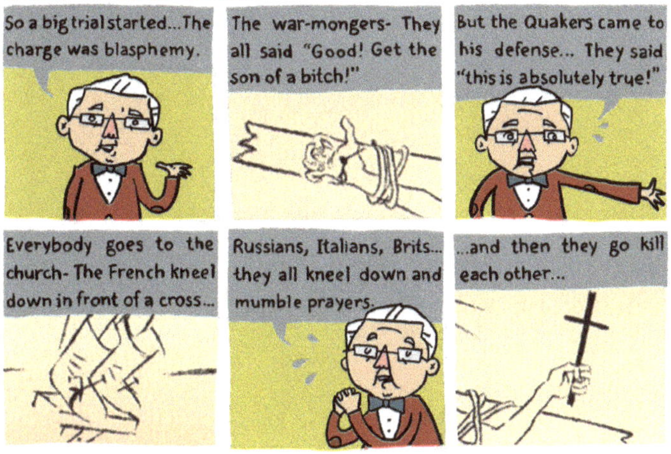
So a big trial started...The charge was blasphemy.
The war-mongers- They all said "Good! Get the son of a bitch!"
But the Quakers came to his defense... They said "this is absolutely true!"
Everybody goes to the church- The French kneel down in front of a cross...
Russians, Italians, Brits... they all kneel down and mumble prayers,
...and then they go kill each other...

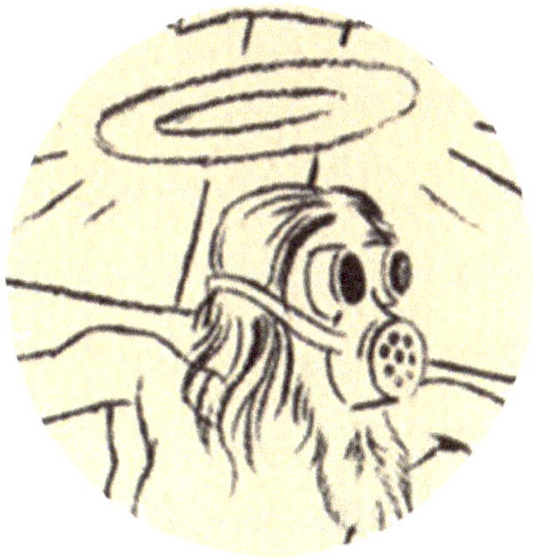

All in the name of "the Prince of Peace"- so called...

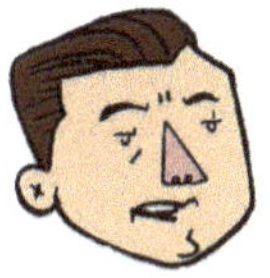

"My work is inconceivable without the times, its horrors, its corruption, its anarchy and its injustice. My intention was to fight against the idea of war, and attack any actions on the part of the Church that lent support to that idea of war."

-from the testimony of George Grosz

A Telegram

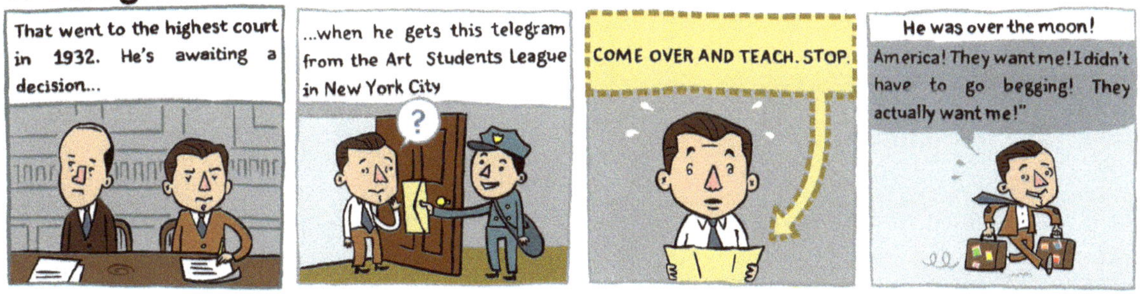
That went to the highest court in 1932. He's awaiting a decision...
...when he gets this telegram from the Art Students League in New York City
?
COME OVER AND TEACH. STOP.
He was over the moon!
America! They want me! I didn't have to go begging! They actually want me!"

At Work in America

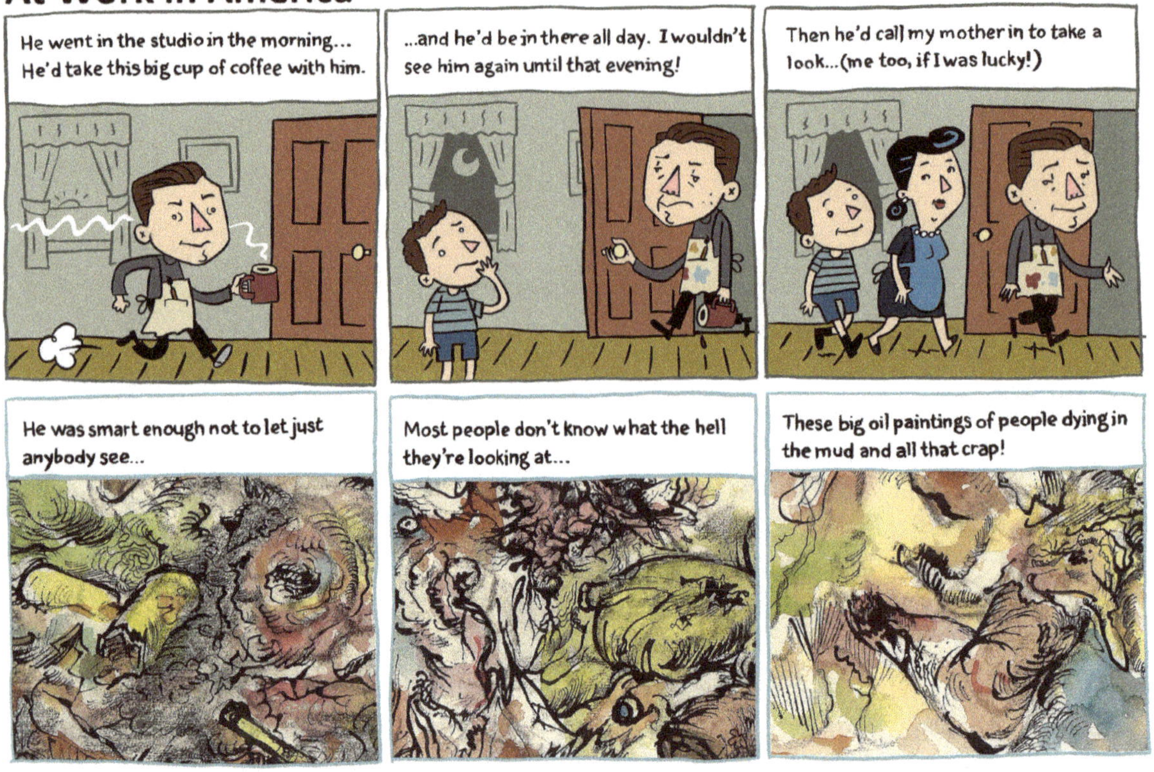

He went in the studio in the morning... He'd take this big cup of coffee with him.
...and he'd be in there all day. I wouldn't see him again until that evening!
Then he'd call my mother in to take a look...(me too, if I was lucky!)
He was smart enough not to let just anybody see...
Most people don't know what the hell they're looking at...
These big oil paintings of people dying in the mud and all that crap!

My Mother

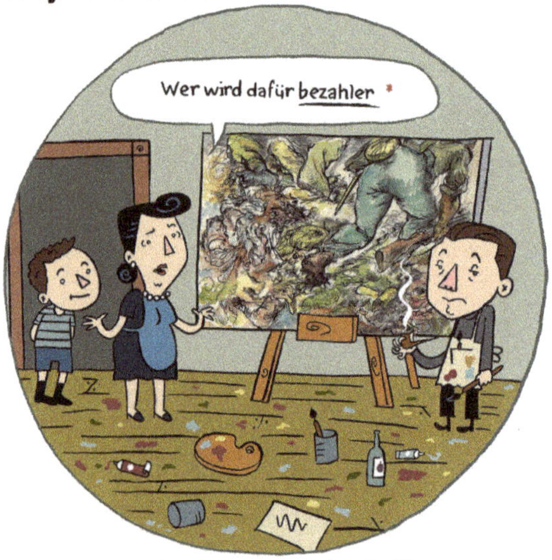

Wer wird dafür bezahlen*

*"Who's going to pay for that?"

A Frequent Guest

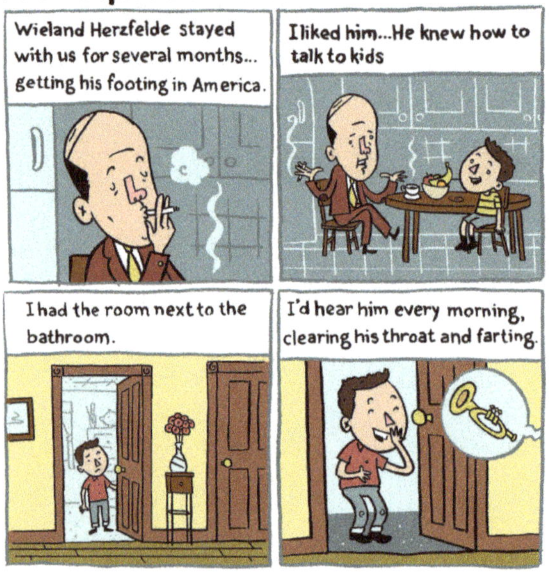

Wieland Herzfelde stayed with us for several months... getting his footing in America.
I liked him...He knew how to talk to kids
I had the room next to the bathroom.
I'd hear him every morning, clearing his throat and farting.

Other Visitors

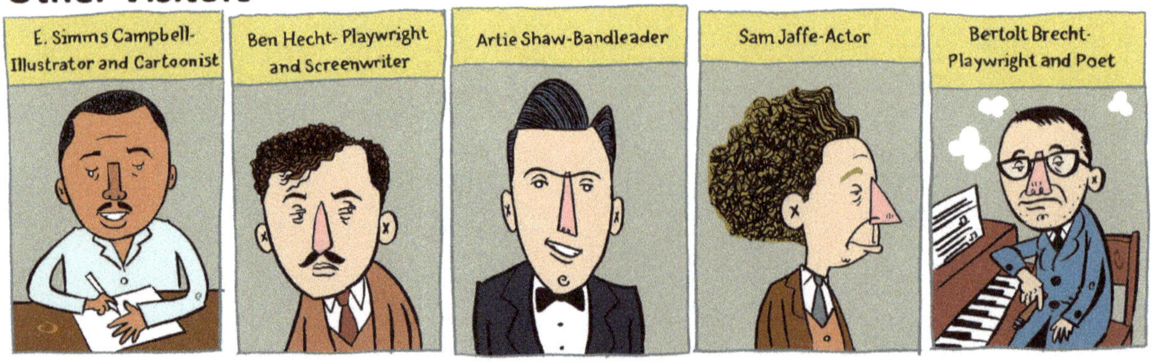

E. Simms Campbell- Illustrator and Cartoonist
Ben Hecht- Playwright and Screenwriter
Artie Shaw-Bandleader
Sam Jaffe-Actor
Bertolt Brecht- Playwright and Poet

*Shit Germany

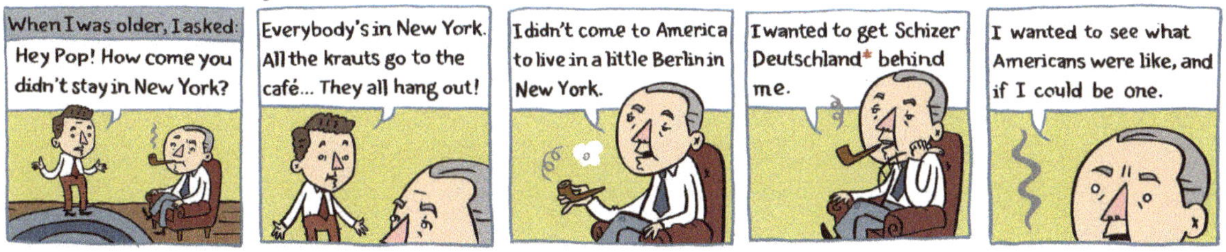
When I was older, I asked:
Hey Pop! How come you didn't stay in New York?
Everybody's in New York. All the krauts go to the café... They all hang out!
I didn't come to America to live in a little Berlin in New York.
I wanted to get Schizer Deutschland* behind me.
I wanted to see what Americans were like, and if I could be one.

"Yes, but is it ART?"

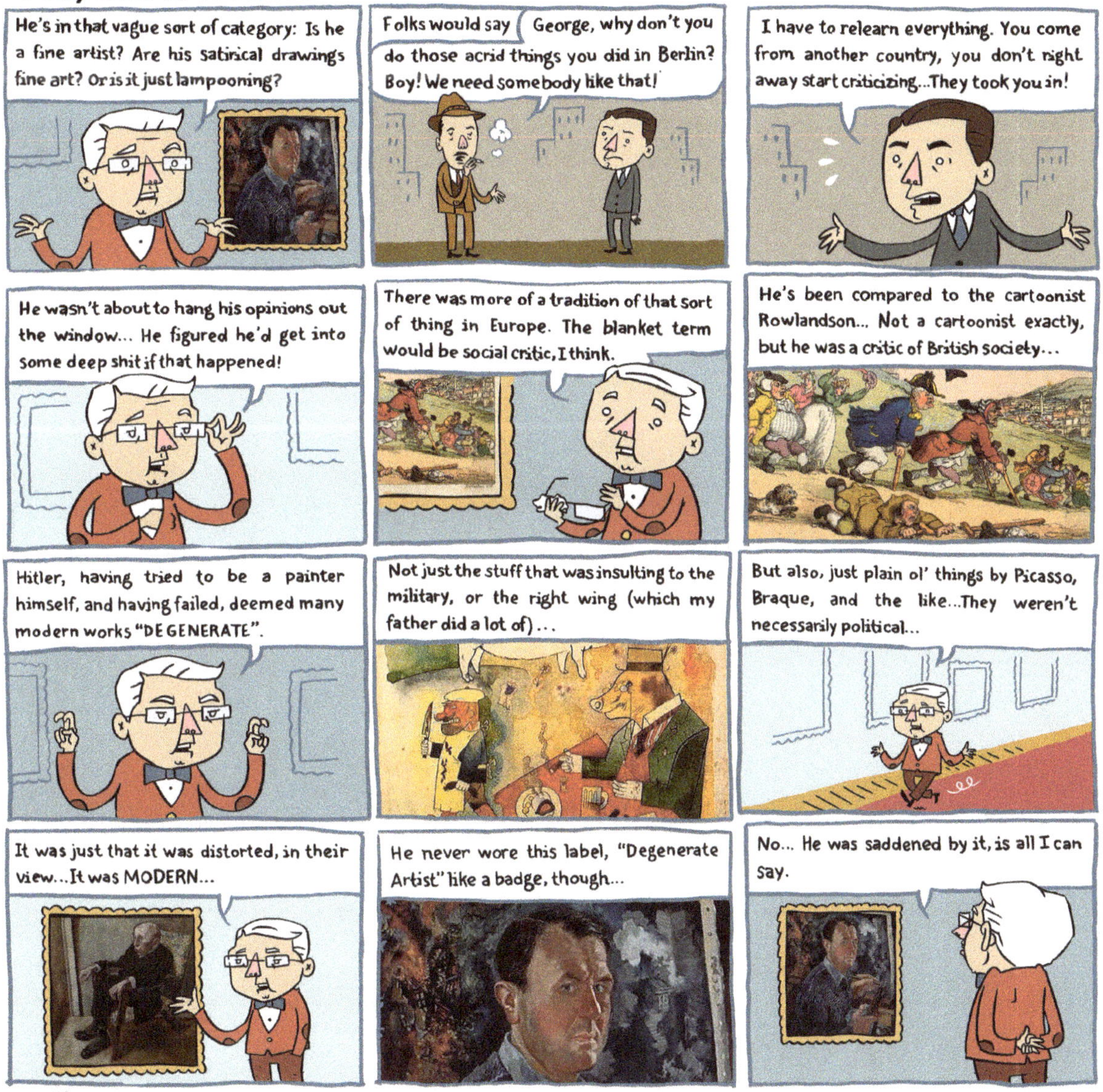
He's in that vague sort of category: Is he a fine artist? Are his satirical drawings fine art? Or is it just lampooning?
Folks would say
George, why don't you do those acrid things you did in Berlin? Boy! We need somebody like that!
I have to relearn everything. You come from another country, you don't right away start criticizing...They took you in!
He wasn't about to hang his opinions out the window... He figured he'd get into some deep shit if that happened!
There was more of a tradition of that sort of thing in Europe. The blanket term would be social critic, I think.
He's been compared to the cartoonist Rowlandson... Not a cartoonist exactly, but he was a critic of British society...
Hitler, having tried to be a painter himself, and having failed, deemed many modern works "DEGENERATE".
Not just the stuff that was insulting to the military, or the right wing (which my father did a lot of)...
But also, just plain ol' things by Picasso, Braque, and the like...They weren't necessarily political...
It was just that it was distorted, in their view...It was MODERN...
He never wore this label, "Degenerate Artist" like a badge, though...
No... He was saddened by it, is all I can say.

epilogue

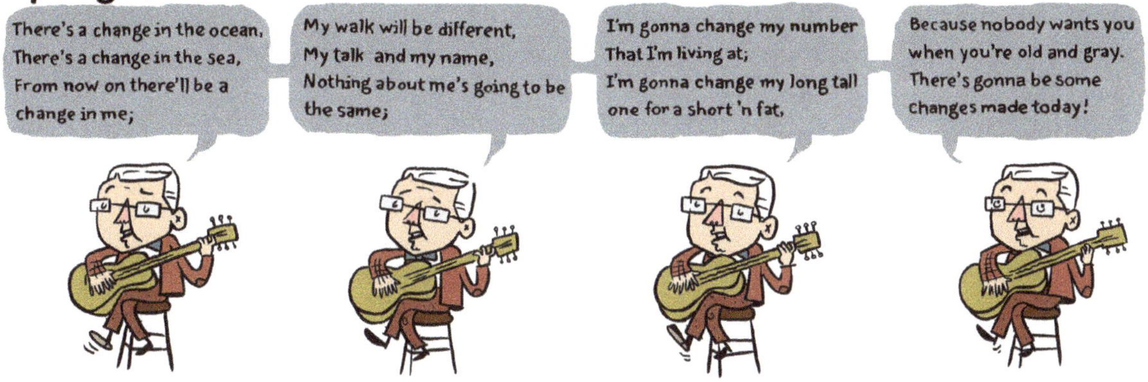
There's a change in the ocean,
There's a change in the sea,
From now on there'll be a change in me;
My walk will be different,
My talk and my name,
Nothing about me's going to be the same;
I'm gonna change my number
That I'm living at;
I'm gonna change my long tall one for a short 'n fat,
Because nobody wants you when you're old and gray.
There's gonna be some changes made today!

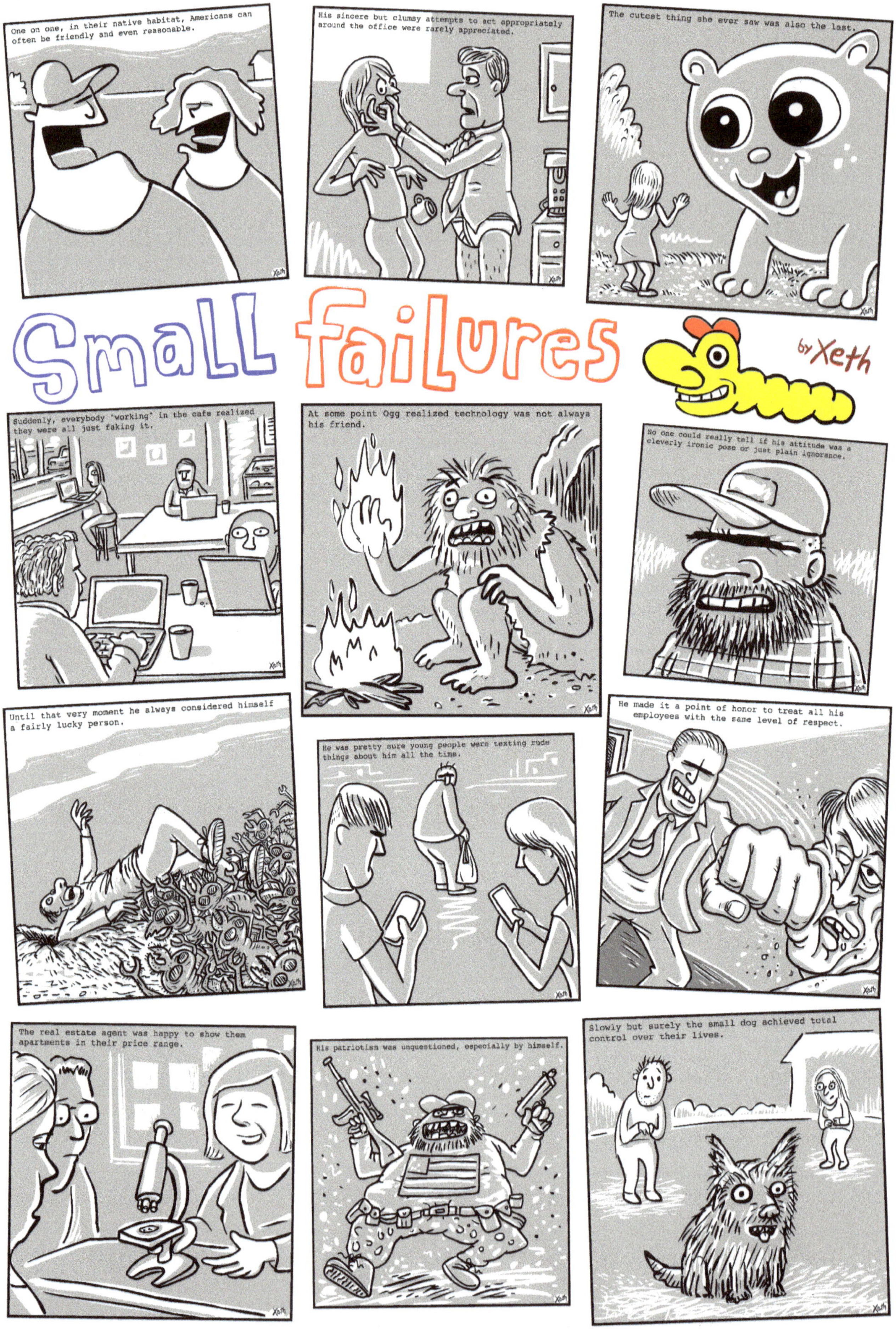

One on one, in their native habitat, Americans can often be friendly and even reasonable.
His sincere but clumsy attempts to act appropriately around the office were rarely appreciated.
The cutest thing she ever saw was also the last.
Small failures
by Xeth
Suddenly, everybody "working" in the cafe realized they were all just faking it.
At some point Ogg realized technology was not always his friend.
No one could really tell if his attitude was a cleverly ironic pose or just plain ignorance.
Until that very moment he always considered himself a fairly lucky person.
He was pretty sure young people were texting rude things about him all the time.
He made it a point of honor to treat all his employees with the same level of respect.
The real estate agent was happy to show them apartments in their price range.
His patriotism was unquestioned, especially by himself.
Slowly but surely the small dog achieved total control over their lives.

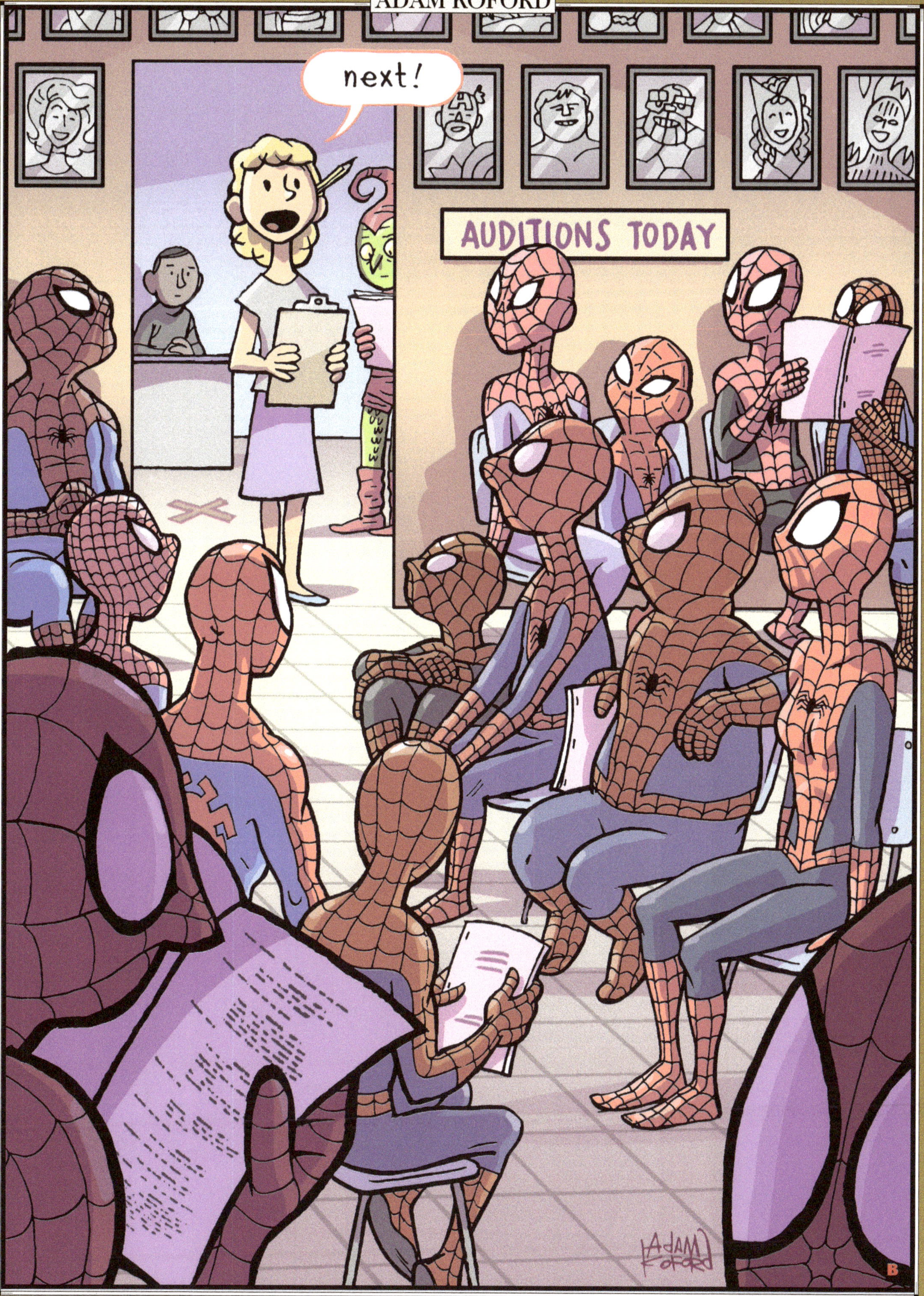
next!
AUDITIONS TODAY
ADAM KOFORD

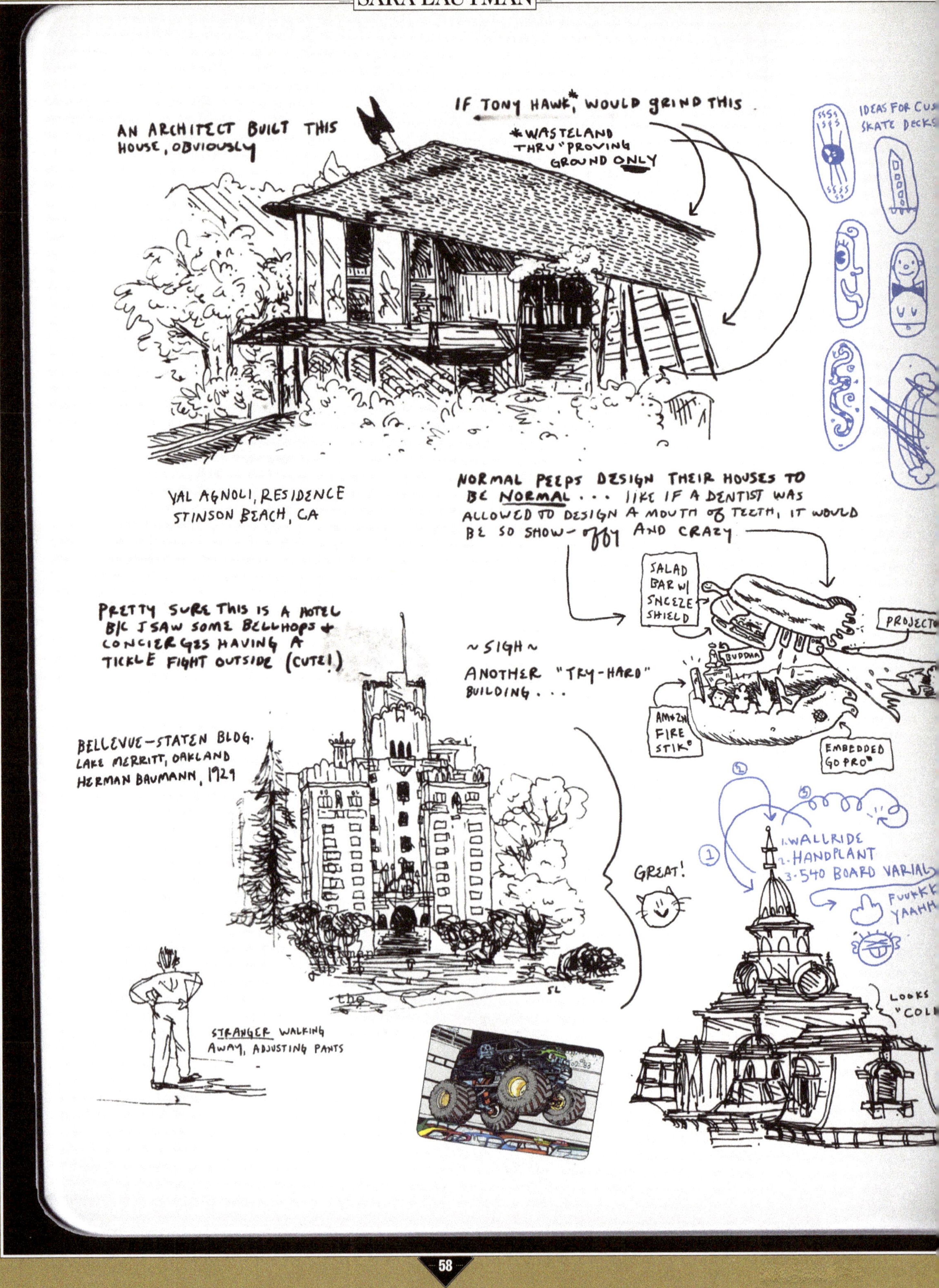
AN ARCHITECT BUILT THIS HOUSE, OBVIOUSLY
IF TONY HAWK* WOULD GRIND THIS
*WASTELAND THRU "PROVING GROUND ONLY
IDEAS FOR CUS
SKATE DECKS
VAL AGNOLI, RESIDENCE
STINSON BEACH, CA
NORMAL PEEPS DESIGN THEIR HOUSES TO BE NORMAL . . . LIKE IF A DENTIST WAS ALLOWED TO DESIGN A MOUTH OF TEETH, IT WOULD BE SO SHOW-OFFY AND CRAZY
SALAD BAR W/ SNEEZE SHIELD
PROJECTO
BUDDHA
AMAZN FIRE STIK®
EMBEDDED GO PRO®
PRETTY SURE THIS IS A HOTEL B/C I SAW SOME BELLHOPS + CONCIERGES HAVING A TICKLE FIGHT OUTSIDE (CUTE!)
~SIGH~
ANOTHER "TRY-HARD" BUILDING . . .
BELLEVUE-STATEN BLDG.
LAKE MERRITT, OAKLAND
HERMAN BAUMANN, 1929
1. WALLRIDE
2. HANDPLANT
3. 540 BOARD VARIAL
FUUKKK YAAHH
GREAT!
SL
LOOKS "COL
STRANGER WALKING AWAY, ADJUSTING PANTS

Architecture Journal

Northern California is home to some of the best buildings in Western architecture. As a summer tourist, it became my daily privilege and practice to wander, taking sketches and absorbing the holistic variety of the landscape.

California makes humanity uncharacteristically eager to cooperate. Beautiful structures are built into the contours of the land. It is illegal to pick, bend, or otherwise hurt California Poppies as they grow on state property. In the face of our staggering ecological damage, such stewardship becomes symbolic (and tragic). May I pick a poppy? No—I am delighted to find—I may not.

Please don't mistake this research for criticism, or (God forbid) scholarship. It is my hope that my visual journals show the legacy of a contented dilettante. —*SL*

ROOF NOT POINTY — AT ALL...? NOT SURE IF COMPLIANT W/ SPIDER MAN FANTASY → EMAIL SOMEONE RE: THIS
SCARY CUPOLA (GHOSTLY WIDOWS OF DEAD SAILORS??) → TOO SCARY!
FLORAL DEPOT BLDG. 18TH + TELEGRAPH ALBERT EVERS, 1931
HC CAPWELL COMPANY
FLOWERS
"FLOWERS"... LOL NICE TRY, MAFIA . . .

THOSE GOOGLE OVERALLS WERE PERFECT MAN I HAD 'EM FOREVER.

CATHEDRAL OF CHRIST THE LIGHT, LAKE MERRITT SHORES, OAKLAND CA
TOO POINTY — DANGEROUS! | UNGRINDABLE?
NEEDS MORE POINTY STUFF ON SIDES — TO WARD OFF THIEVES

HEARD THERE WAS A BIG SECRET WOMEN-ONLY TRAMPOLINE PARK UP HERE OWNED BY FACEBOOK
DREW THIS FROM A PHOTOGRAPH SO NO WAY TO CONFIRM WHETHER IT ACTUALLY EXISTS OR NOT...
THIS BUILDING DEF EXISTS — DRAWN FROM LIFE! (WINK!)
IF TONY HAWK* WOULD GRIND RAILS HERE
* PRO SKATER 5 AND EARLIER ONLY
SUMITOMO BANK FRANKLIN + 20TH SHIGENURI IYAMA

Please Tell Me You Love Me

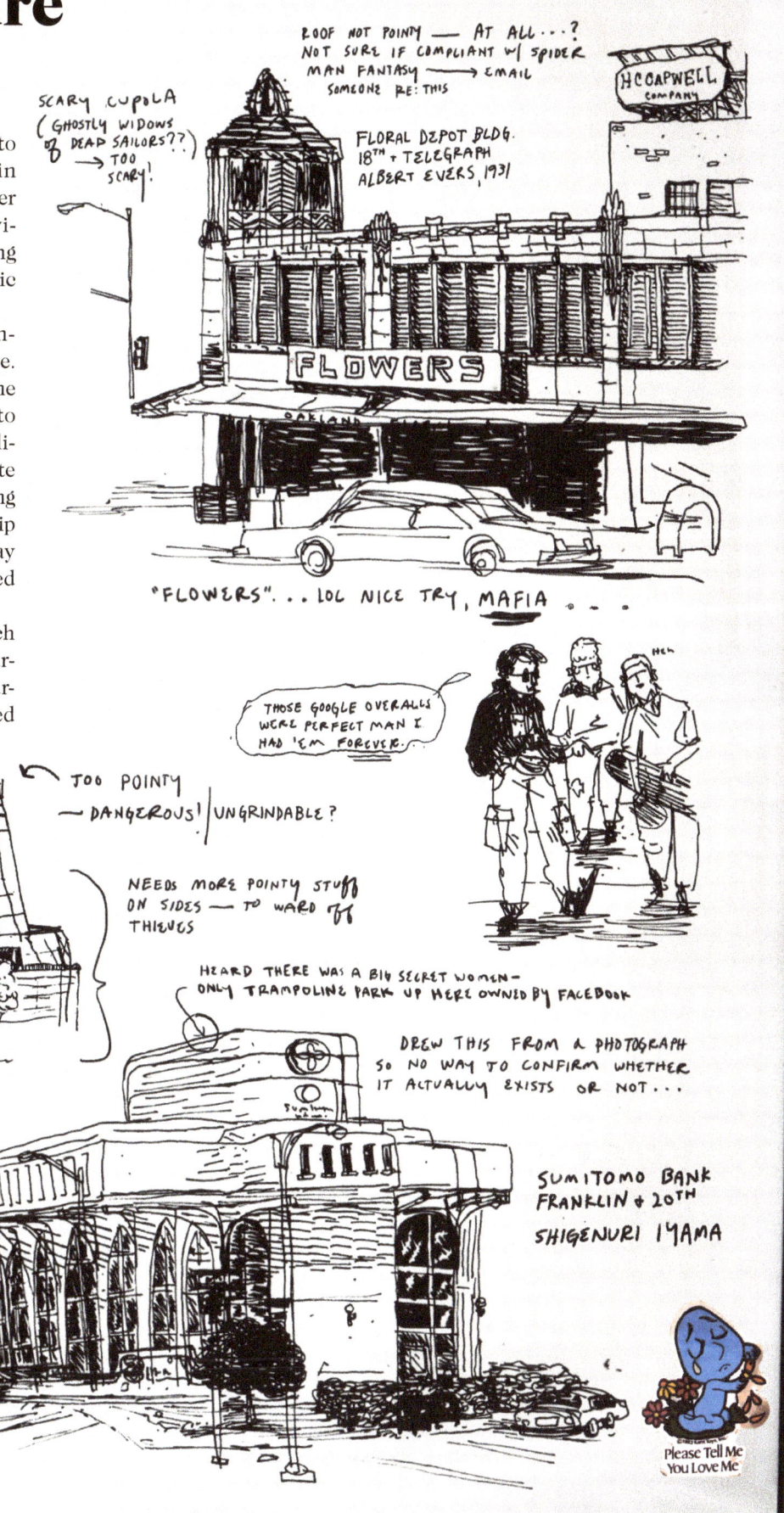

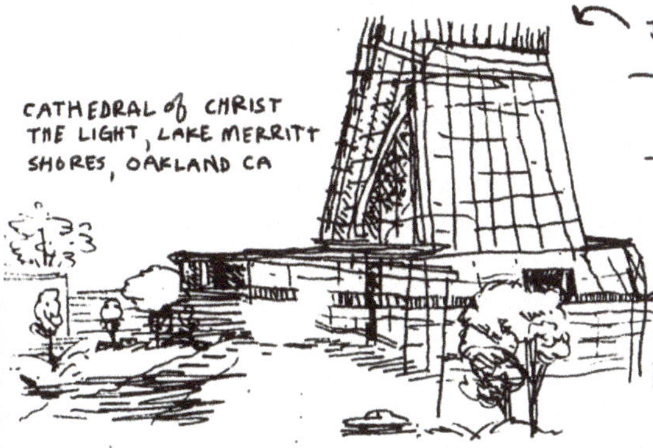

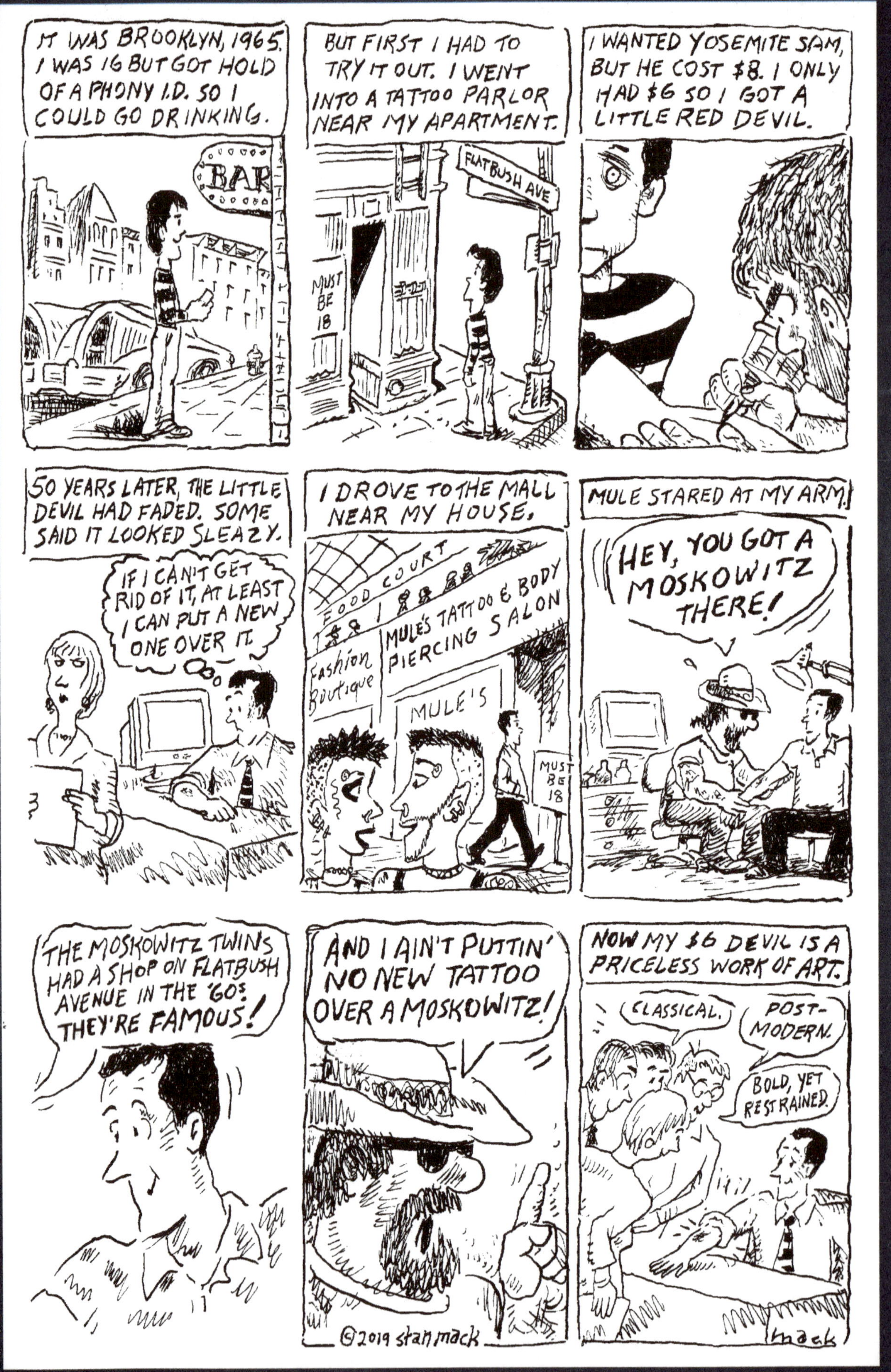
IT WAS BROOKLYN, 1965. I WAS 16 BUT GOT HOLD OF A PHONY I.D. SO I COULD GO DRINKING.
BAR
BUT FIRST I HAD TO TRY IT OUT. I WENT INTO A TATTOO PARLOR NEAR MY APARTMENT.
FLATBUSH AVE
MUST BE 18
I WANTED YOSEMITE SAM, BUT HE COST $8. I ONLY HAD $6 SO I GOT A LITTLE RED DEVIL.
50 YEARS LATER, THE LITTLE DEVIL HAD FADED. SOME SAID IT LOOKED SLEAZY.
IF I CAN'T GET RID OF IT, AT LEAST I CAN PUT A NEW ONE OVER IT.
I DROVE TO THE MALL NEAR MY HOUSE.
FOOD COURT
MULE'S TATTOO & BODY PIERCING SALON
Fashion Boutique
MULE'S
MUST BE 18
MULE STARED AT MY ARM.
HEY, YOU GOT A MOSKOWITZ THERE!
THE MOSKOWITZ TWINS HAD A SHOP ON FLATBUSH AVENUE IN THE '60s. THEY'RE FAMOUS!
AND I AIN'T PUTTIN' NO NEW TATTOO OVER A MOSKOWITZ!
©2019 stan mack
NOW MY $6 DEVIL IS A PRICELESS WORK OF ART.
CLASSICAL.
POST-MODERN.
BOLD, YET RESTRAINED.
mack

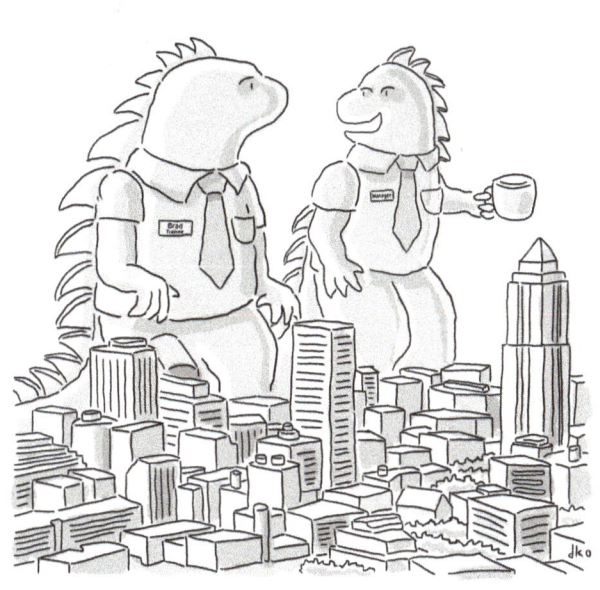

"Easy there, Sinatra. First let's see what you can do with Des Moines."

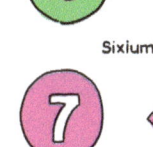

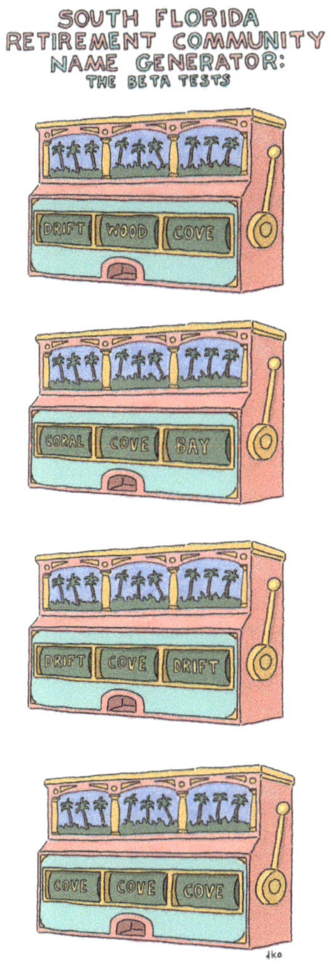

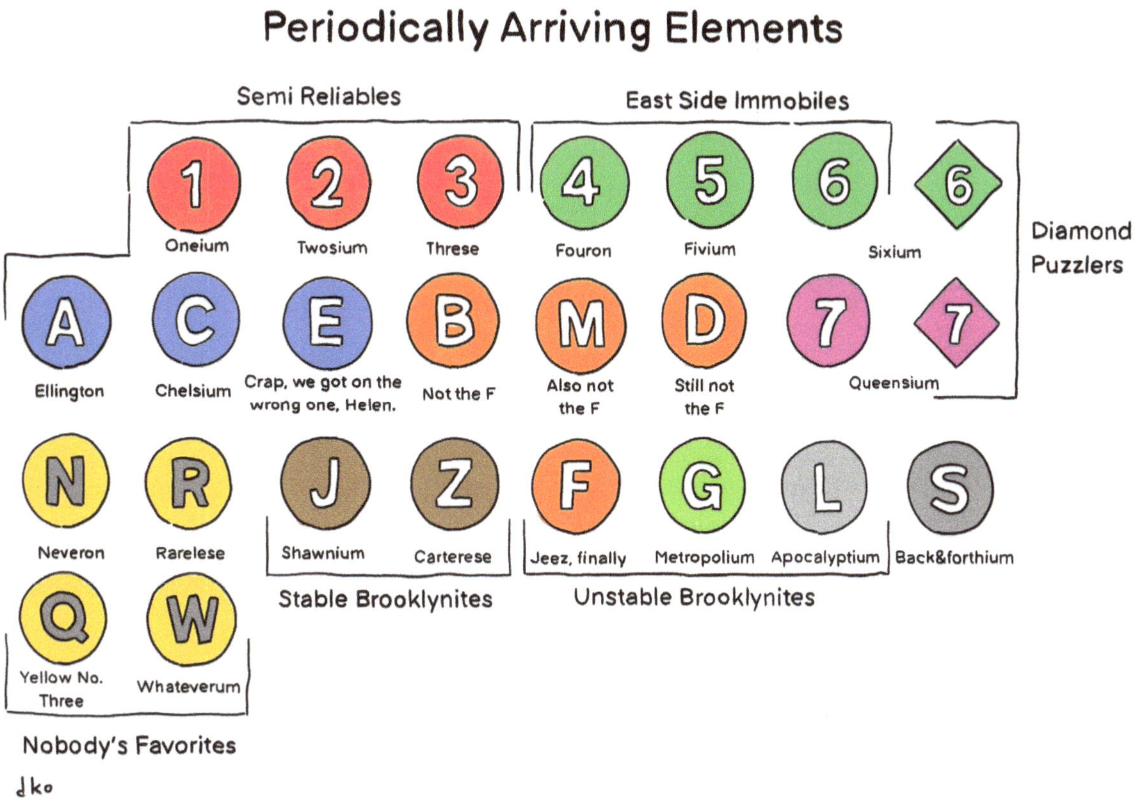

SOUTH FLORIDA RETIREMENT COMMUNITY NAME GENERATOR:
THE BETA TESTS
DRIFT WOOD COVE
CORAL COVE BAY
DRIFT COVE DRIFT
COVE COVE COVE

Periodically Arriving Elements
Semi Reliables
1 Oneium
2 Twosium
3 Threse
East Side Immobiles
4 Fouron
5 Fivium
6 Sixium
Diamond Puzzlers
A Ellington
C Chelsium
E Crap, we got on the wrong one, Helen.
B Not the F
M Also not the F
D Still not the F
7 Queensium
N Neveron
R Rarelese
J Shawnium
Z Carterese
Stable Brooklynites
F Jeez, finally
G Metropolium
L Apocalyptium
S Back&forthium
Unstable Brooklynites
Q Yellow No. Three
W Whateverum
Nobody's Favorites

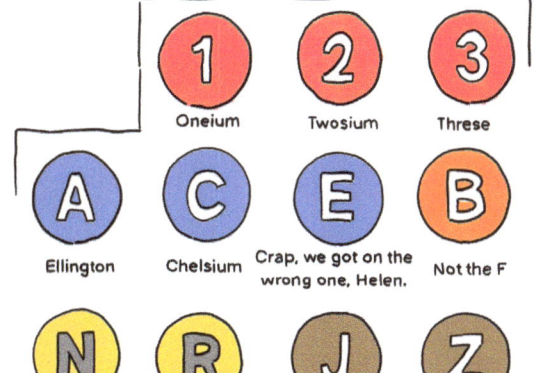

The Red Menace

Someone asked Harold Ross why he didn't print cartoons in color. "What's so funny about red?" he replied.

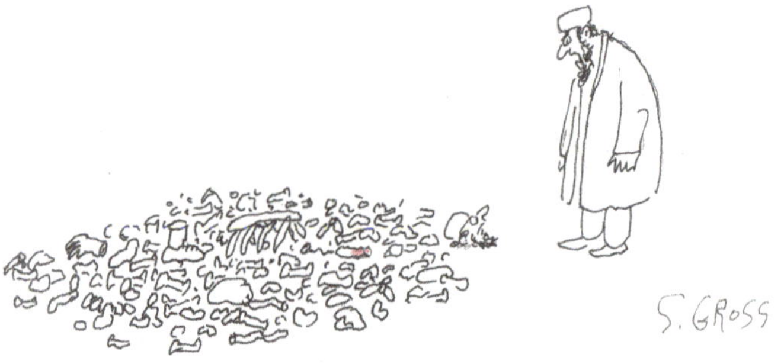
S. GROSS

"No virgins for you! You never told me you were transgendered!"

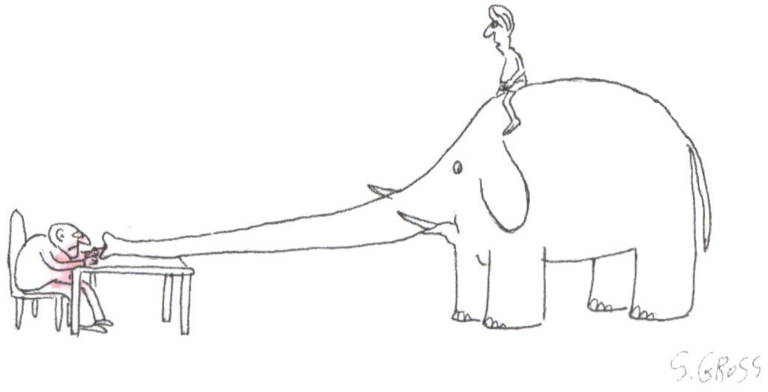
S. GROSS

"She suffers from nosebleeds, doctor."

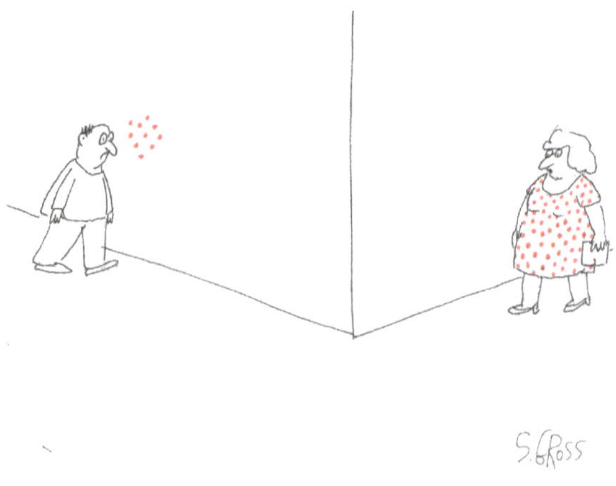
S. GROSS

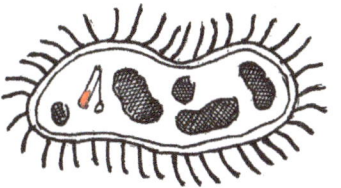

"What have you done with Mrs. Parkhurst?"

"I TOLD you not to touch it!"

"What's going on? I was taking a shower and the water turned into wine."

CARTOONISTS IN CARS GETTING AGITA

by Bob Eckstein and Nick Downes

This is a 2012 Mini Cooper Clubman in pepper white with black hardtop and side walls. It has rally race numbers and white racing stripes. The Clubman has THREE doors
29
and an unusual barn-door in the back. Under the bonnet is a turbo181 horsepower 1.6 liter four-cylinder BMW engine.
The interior is a modified retro dashboard in red leather and faux wood with checkered pattern starter button and controls. White leather seats and side panels. For the driver, a rare 1950s German leather steering wheel. The car's interior lights are programmed to change colors according to mood and there are at least two James Bond-like secret compartments.
All of this is very British and perfect for my next guest, renown cartoonist Nick Downes, who is often mistaken for being British as his work is beloved in England – á la Jerry Lewis in France.
Nick Downes
His most famous cartoon is this one from *Nat'l Lampoon...*
"I'm sorry you saw me, Timmy. Now I'll have to kill you."
Nick also being a steak guy, agreed we try the Resorts World Casino Prime Steak House in Queens where we would cash in on a $100 comp I got for my online gambling problem.
So does the 29 [on the side of the car] mean anything?
My Dad passed away unexpectedly the same day I got the Mini. Cars were our one common interest. I learned at the funeral he had a gambling problem and that 29, his birthday, was his lucky number. Then I later found out it was pretty UNlucky for him. Nevertheless, it's there in his memory.
We first strolled thru the adjacent legendary Aqueduct Racetrack. It's not the dump we expected.
While on our way to the restaurant to spend $100 on steaks, I hit a $100 jackpot on the penny slots.
TRIPLE
I knew a guy who spent many months perfecting a sure-fire card counting system.
No, I mean that literally - hit me.
When he was ready, he sat down at a blackjack table in Lake Tahoe and ordered a drink. Before a card was dealt, he bit down on an ice cube that wasn't, and spit out a bloody shard of glass.
He quickly settled with the casino for more than he ever could have made with his cockamamie card scheme.
Resorts World CASINO
Whatever happened to the guy?
He was busted leaving a Las Vegas furrier's, wearing a full-length mink coat under his shirt and pants.
29
Nick, I think I tipped our waiteress that $100 bill.
So we broke even.

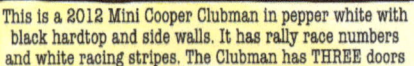

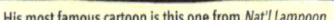

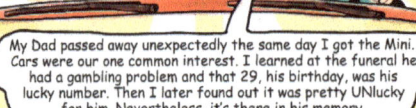

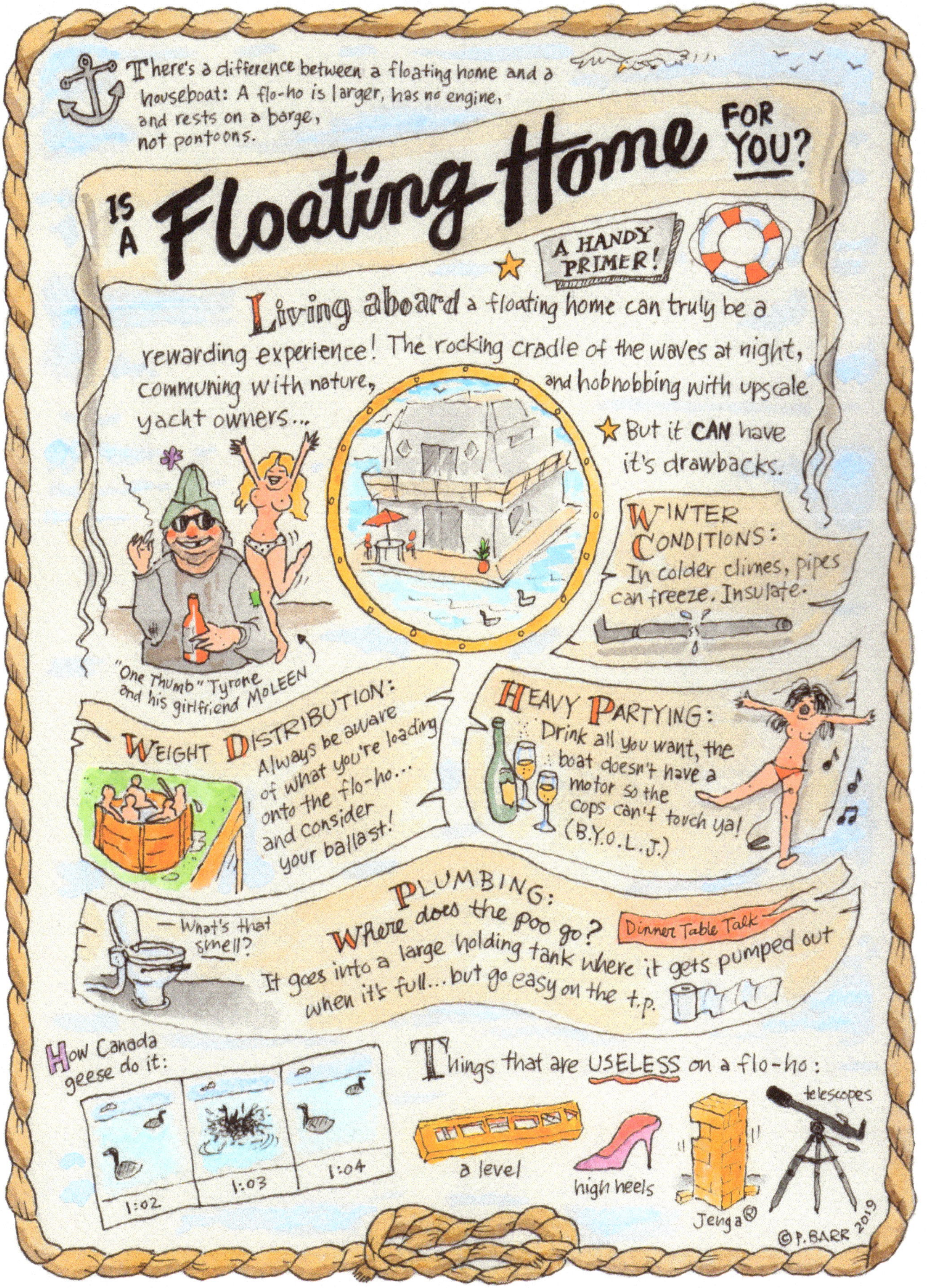
There's a difference between a floating home and a houseboat: A flo-ho is larger, has no engine, and rests on a barge, not pontoons.
IS A Floating Home FOR YOU?
A HANDY PRIMER!
Living aboard a floating home can truly be a rewarding experience! The rocking cradle of the waves at night, communing with nature, and hobnobbing with upscale yacht owners...
But it CAN have it's drawbacks.
"One Thumb" Tyrone and his girlfriend MoLEEN
WINTER CONDITIONS: In colder climes, pipes can freeze. Insulate.
WEIGHT DISTRIBUTION: Always be aware of what you're loading onto the flo-ho... and consider your ballast!
HEAVY PARTYING: Drink all you want, the boat doesn't have a motor so the cops can't touch ya! (B.Y.O.L.J.)
PLUMBING: Where does the poo go?
Dinner Table Talk
— What's that smell?
It goes into a large holding tank where it gets pumped out when it's full... but go easy on the t.p.
How Canada geese do it:
1:02
1:03
1:04
Things that are USELESS on a flo-ho:
a level
high heels
Jenga®
telescopes
©P. BARR 2019

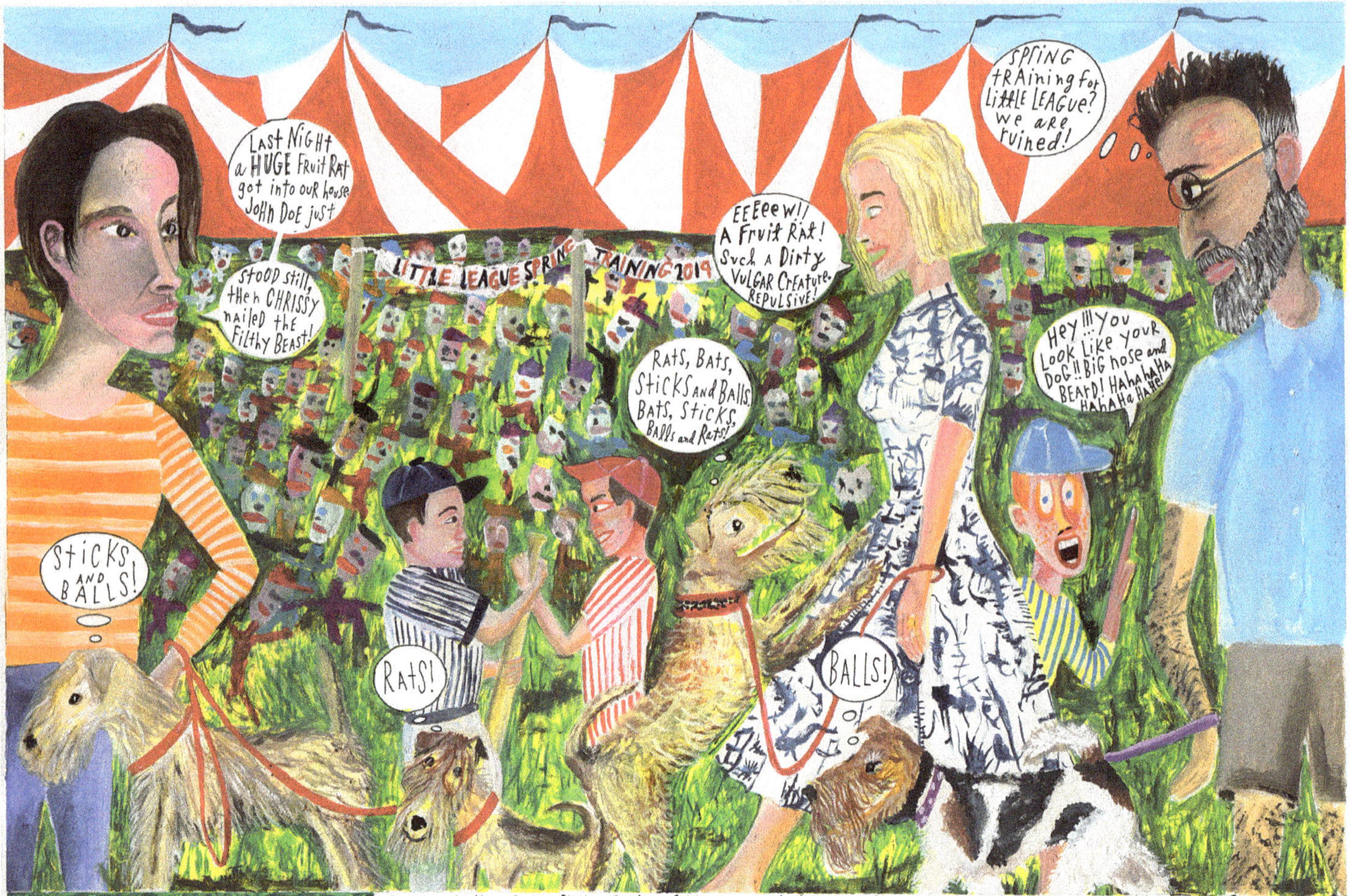
Last Night a HUGE Fruit Rat got into our house. John Doe just stood still, then CHRISSY nailed the Filthy Beast!
STICKS AND BALLS!
EEEeew!! A Fruit Rat! Such a Dirty VULGAR Creature. REPULSIVE!
Rats, Bats, Sticks and Balls Bats, Sticks Balls and Rats!
Rats!
BALLS!
Spring training for Little League? We are ruined!
Hey!!! You look like your Dog!! Big nose and BEARD!

The WASPS

No, this isn't a comic strip version of the play by Aristophanes, nor is it a satirical essay about Pilgrims, Plymouth Rock and all that jazz. It doesn't take place in Ancient Greece in 422 BC, and it most certainly didn't go down in the year 1620 by a boulder on the shingle of the future Commonwealth of Massachusetts. Every spring, Phoenix hosts spring training for the Cactus League of major league baseball. Fans come from all over to watch their favorite teams and enjoy beautiful weather. Early one morning this past spring break, my wife and I were walking our terriers with a friend who is also a terrier fan. Strolling through an enormous park, we were stunned to discover Little League Spring Training! The numerous baseball fields were filled with teams, coaches, parents and others milling about in the low thousands. Suddenly, I was flush with humiliation.

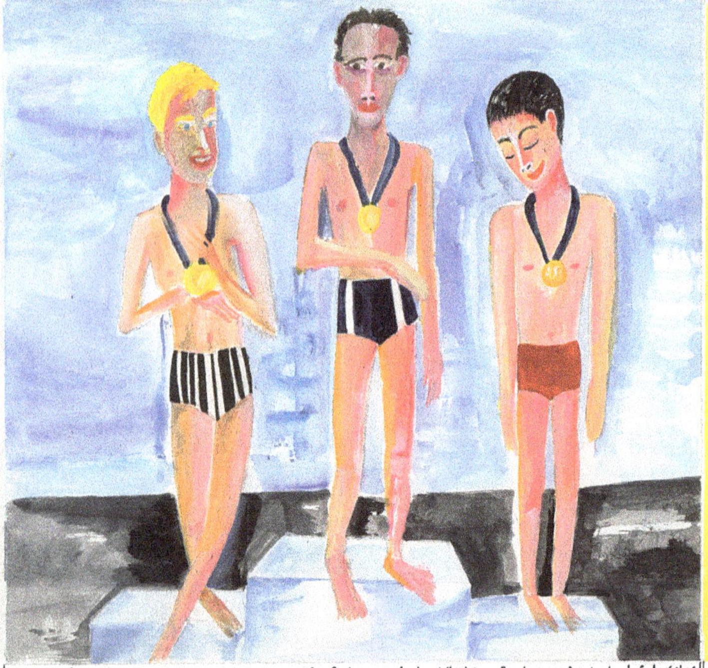

Bewildered by the sight of it, my mind leapt into the Way-Back machine to Los Angeles during the late 1960's to my own Little League experience as a bench warming member of what was arguably one of the worst teams in Little League history, the WASPS. At the time, I was on a swim team that was winning. Somehow, someone, most likely a meddlesome parent, convinced our coach of the idea to try forming a baseball team.

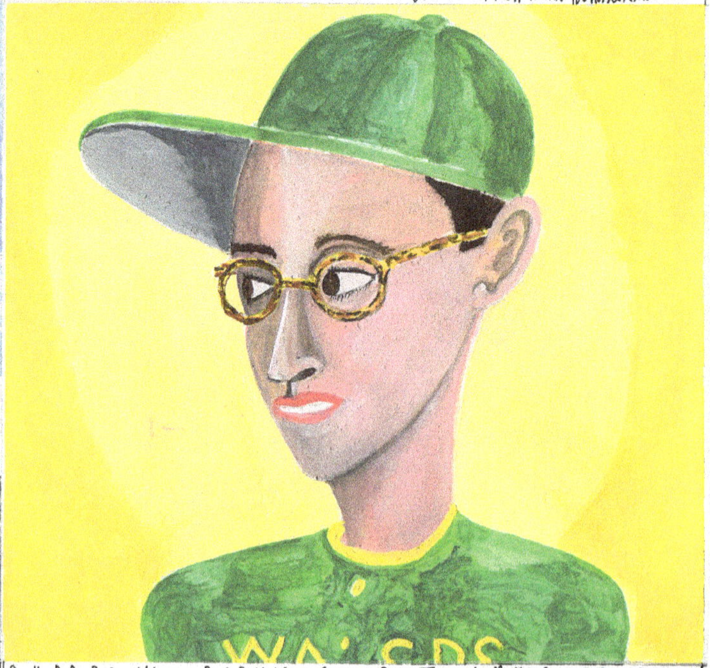

So he did. Recruiting a baseball team from a swim team isn't the brightest of ideas. While technically speaking both things are teams, swimming is essentially a solitary activity where one's main competitor is oneself. It is concerned with form, timing and speed. The interactivity and interdependency present in baseball are absent. The sport of swimming has far more in common with horseracing, a different animal entirely.

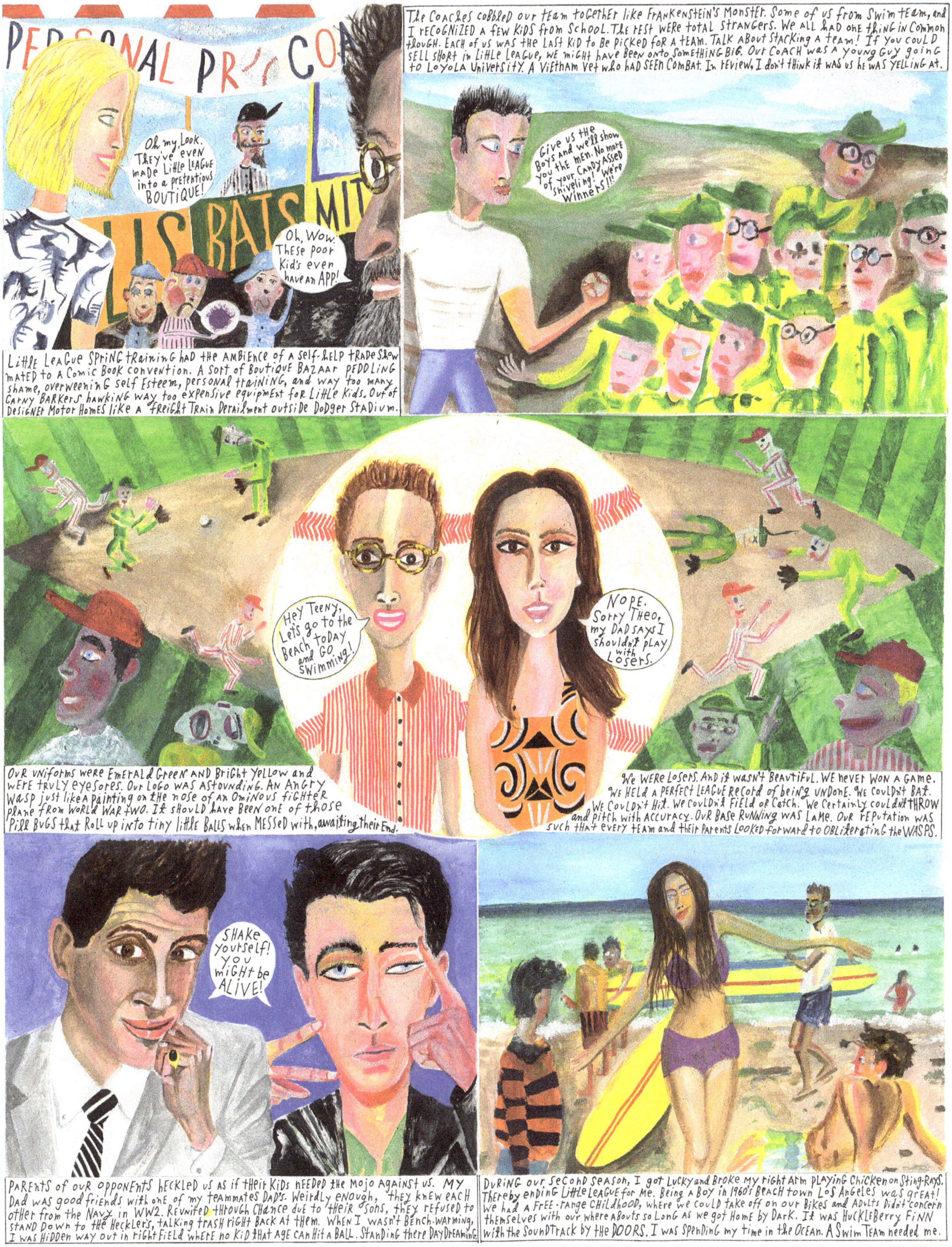
Oh my. Look. They've even made Little League into a pretentious BOUTIQUE!
Oh, Wow. These poor Kid's even have an APP!
Little League Spring training had the ambience of a self-help trade show mated to a Comic Book convention. A sort of Boutique Bazaar peddling shame, overweening self esteem, personal training, and way too many Carny Barkers hawking way too expensive equipment for Little Kids. Out of Designer Motor Homes like a Freight Train Derailment outside Dodger Stadium.
The Coaches cobbled our team together like Frankenstein's Monster. Some of us from Swim team, and I recognized a few kids from School. The rest were total strangers. We all had one thing in common though. Each of us was the last kid to be picked for a team. Talk about stacking a team! If you could sell short in Little League, we might have been onto something big. Our coach was a young guy going to Loyola University. A Vietnam vet who had seen combat. In review, I don't think it was us he was yelling at.
Give us the Boys and we'll show you the men. No more of your Candy Assed Sniveling! We're Winners!!!
Hey Teeny, Let's go to the Beach today and go swimming!
Nope. Sorry Theo, my Dad says I shouldn't play with Losers.
Our uniforms were Emerald Green and Bright Yellow and were truly eyesores. Our logo was astounding. An Angry Wasp just like a painting on the nose of an Ominous fighter plane from World War two. It should have been one of those Pill Bugs that roll up into tiny little balls when messed with, awaiting their End.
We were losers. And it wasn't beautiful. We never won a game. We held a perfect League record of being undone. We couldn't bat. We couldn't hit. We couldn't field or catch. We certainly couldn't throw and pitch with accuracy. Our base running was lame. Our reputation was such that every team and their parents looked forward to obliterating the WASPS.
SHAKE yourself! you might be ALIVE!
Parents of our opponents heckled us as if their kids needed the mojo against us. My Dad was good friends with one of my teammates Dad's. Weirdly enough, they knew each other from the Navy in WW2. Reunited through chance due to their sons, they refused to stand down to the Heckler's, talking trash right back at them. When I wasn't Bench-warming, I was hidden way out in right field where no kid that age can hit a ball. Standing there daydreaming.
During our second season, I got lucky and broke my right arm playing chicken on Sting-Rays. Thereby ending Little League for me. Being a Boy in 1960's Beach town Los Angeles was great! We had a free-range childhood, where we could take off on our bikes and adults didn't concern themselves with our whereabouts so long as we got home by dark. It was Huckleberry Finn with the soundtrack by the Doors. I was spending my time in the Ocean. A Swim Team needed me.

NEW FROM FANTAGRAPHICS UNDERGROUND

"For 50-plus years, wherever the action, Mort's been front-and-center—a gimlet-eyed observer and artful insta-chronicler of our times, as fluent outside the box as, in our pages, drawing within it."

—Emma Allen
Cartoon Editor, *The New Yorker*

MORT GERBERG
ON THE SCENE
A 50-Year Cartoon Chronicle

Mort Gerberg's social-justice-minded — and bitingly funny — cartoons have appeared in magazines such as *The Realist*, *The New Yorker*, *Playboy*, and the *Saturday Evening Post*. And as a reporter, he's sketched historic scenes like the fiery Women's Marches of the '60s and the infamous '68 Democratic National Convention. Fantagraphics Underground is proud to present a 50-year career retrospective of this vital cartoonist, collecting his magazine cartoons, sketchbook drawings, and on-the-scene reportage sketches in one handsome volume.

AVAILABLE NOW AT FANTAGRAPHICS.COM

P.S. MUELLER THINKS LIKE THIS

The cartoonist/broadcaster/writer is always walking around, looking at stuff • **By P.S. Mueller**

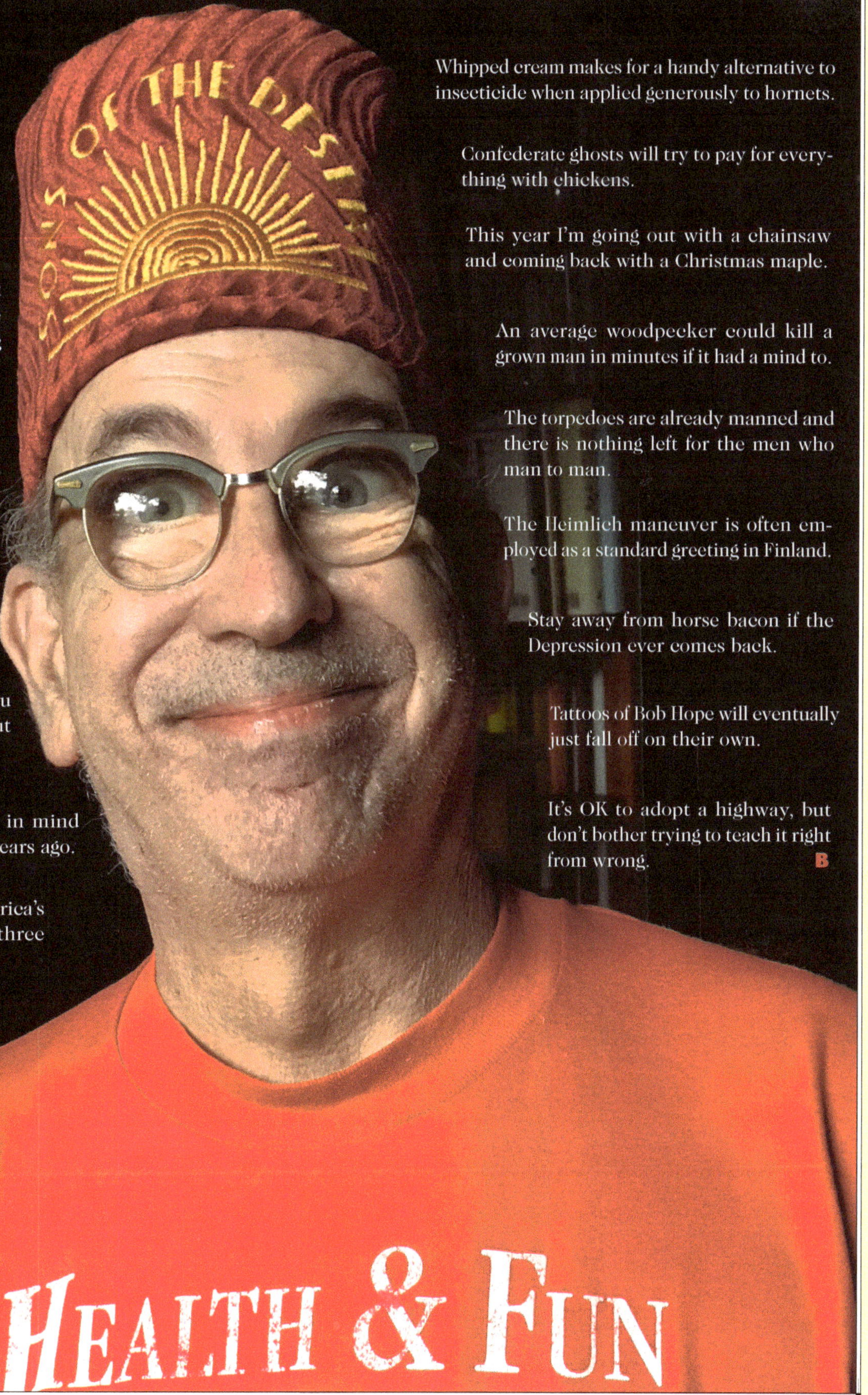
HEALTH & FUN

You can get a lot more out of life if you lie on the application.

Raisin pie was never a good idea and never will be.

The great thing about winter is you have time to save up before burying your dead.

The color yellow will retire soon. Enjoy it while you can.

Cowboys, it's really time to change that cow litter.

Talking dogs are fine if you want to hear a lot about bones.

Carnival barkers, keep in mind that I stepped right up years ago.

People living along America's coastlines should take three steps back.

The aging process will only get you so far.

Whipped cream makes for a handy alternative to insecticide when applied generously to hornets.

Confederate ghosts will try to pay for everything with chickens.

This year I'm going out with a chainsaw and coming back with a Christmas maple.

An average woodpecker could kill a grown man in minutes if it had a mind to.

The torpedoes are already manned and there is nothing left for the men who man to man.

The Heimlich maneuver is often employed as a standard greeting in Finland.

Stay away from horse bacon if the Depression ever comes back.

Tattoos of Bob Hope will eventually just fall off on their own.

It's OK to adopt a highway, but don't bother trying to teach it right from wrong. B

TIME-TRAVEL STUDY BUDDIES

In this episode, Lucy & José meet Roman general Julius Caesar! • **By Simon Rich & Farley Katz**

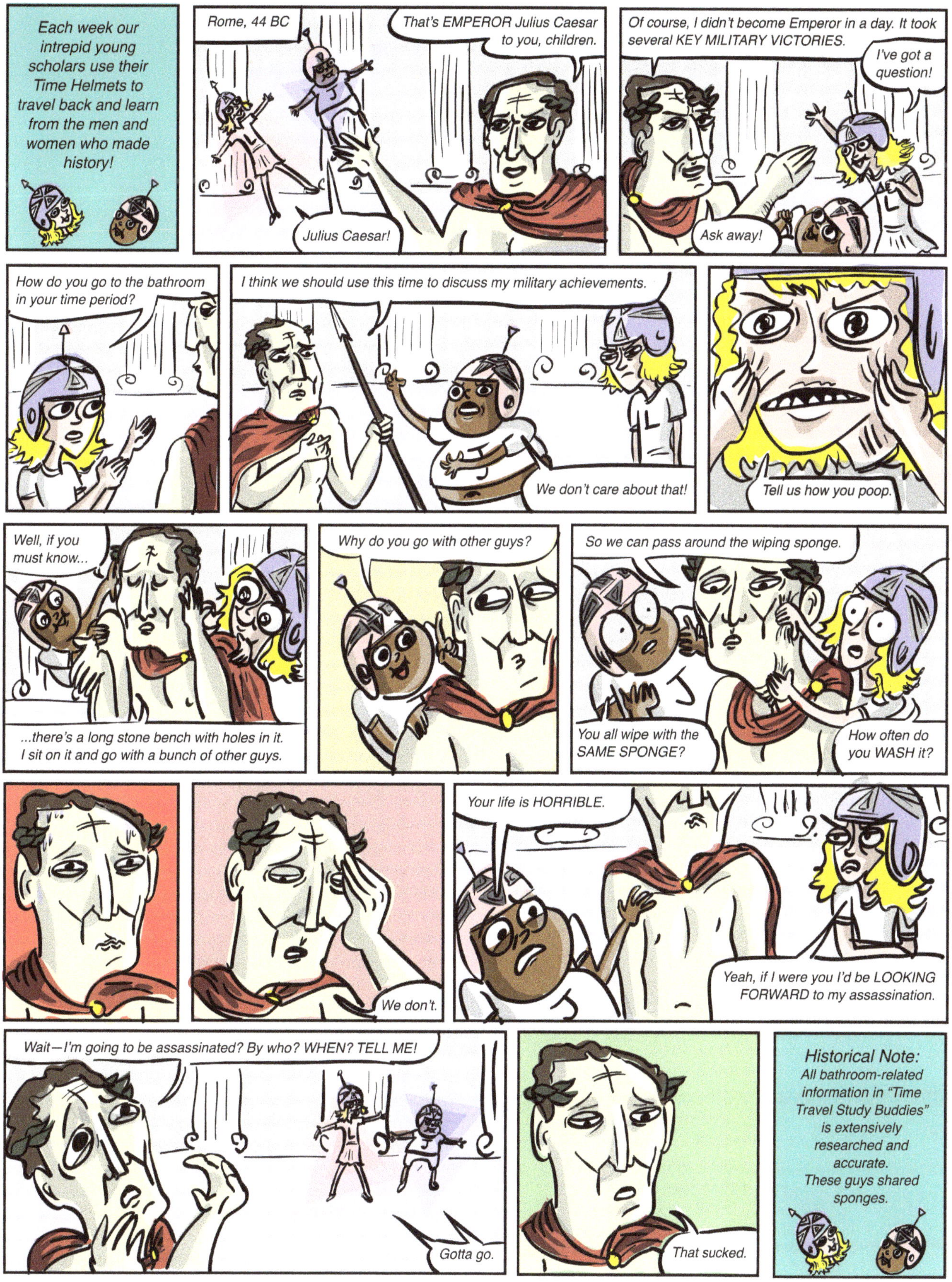
Each week our intrepid young scholars use their Time Helmets to travel back and learn from the men and women who made history!
Rome, 44 BC
Julius Caesar!
That's EMPEROR Julius Caesar to you, children.
Of course, I didn't become Emperor in a day. It took several KEY MILITARY VICTORIES.
I've got a question!
Ask away!
How do you go to the bathroom in your time period?
I think we should use this time to discuss my military achievements.
We don't care about that!
Tell us how you poop.
Well, if you must know...
...there's a long stone bench with holes in it. I sit on it and go with a bunch of other guys.
Why do you go with other guys?
So we can pass around the wiping sponge.
You all wipe with the SAME SPONGE?
How often do you WASH it?
We don't.
Your life is HORRIBLE.
Yeah, if I were you I'd be LOOKING FORWARD to my assassination.
Wait—I'm going to be assassinated? By who? WHEN? TELL ME!
Gotta go.
That sucked.
Historical Note:
All bathroom-related information in "Time Travel Study Buddies" is extensively researched and accurate.
These guys shared sponges.

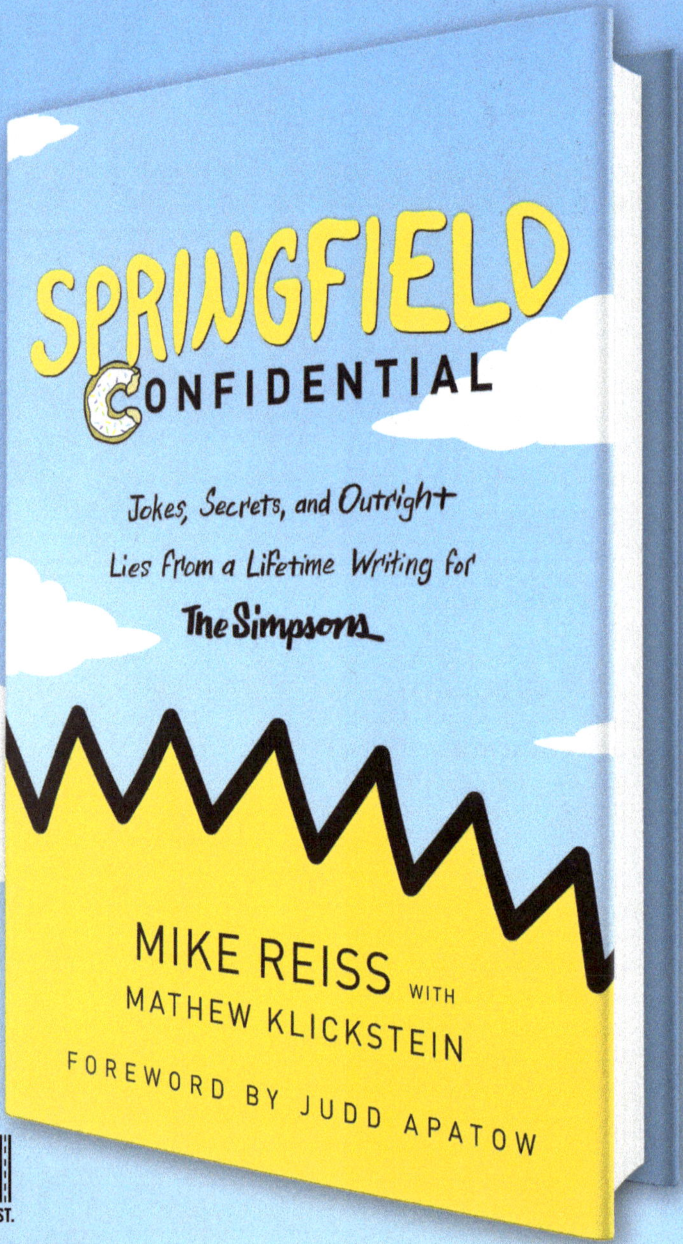

SPRINGFIELD CONFIDENTIAL

JOKES, SECRETS, AND OUTRIGHT LIES FROM A LIFETIME WRITING FOR

The Simpsons

"A truly great comic is rare. Mike Reiss, by definition, is a rarity." —CONAN O'BRIEN

In celebration of *The Simpsons* 30th anniversary, the show's longest-serving writer and producer shares stories, scandals, and gossip about working with AMERICA'S MOST ICONIC CARTOON FAMILY.

Featuring interviews with JUDD APATOW, CONAN O'BRIEN, and *Simpsons* legends AL JEAN, NANCY CARTWRIGHT, DAN CASTELLANETA, and more!

ON SALE NOW

MIKE REISS with MATHEW KLICKSTEIN
FOREWORD BY JUDD APATOW

DEY ST.
www.hc.com

WHAT AM I DOING HERE?

Animals have so much to teach us, if we would only listen. • ***By Mike Reiss***

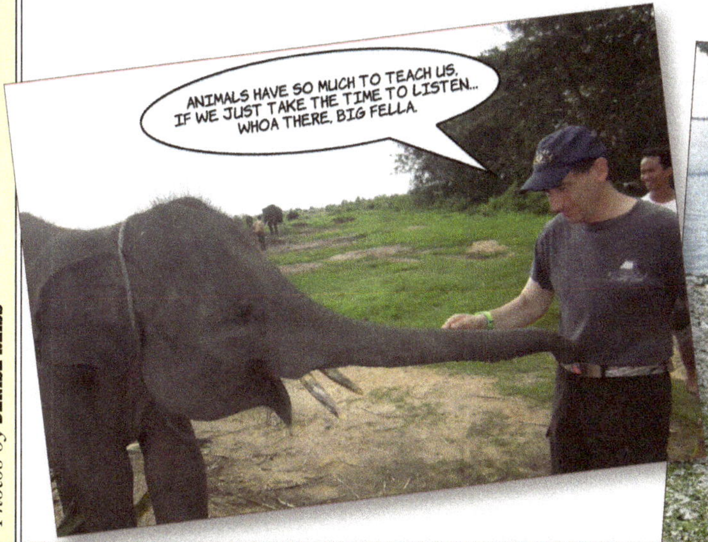
ANIMALS HAVE SO MUCH TO TEACH US, IF WE JUST TAKE THE TIME TO LISTEN... WHOA THERE, BIG FELLA.

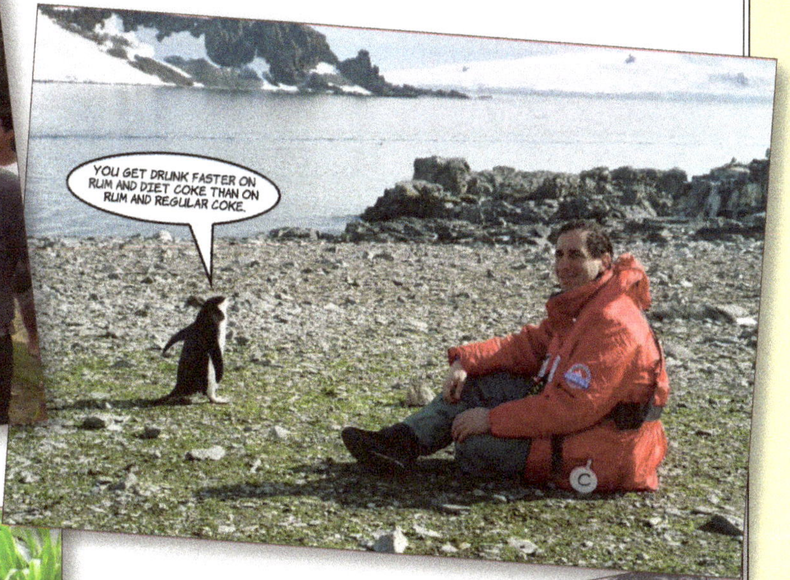
YOU GET DRUNK FASTER ON RUM AND DIET COKE THAN ON RUM AND REGULAR COKE.

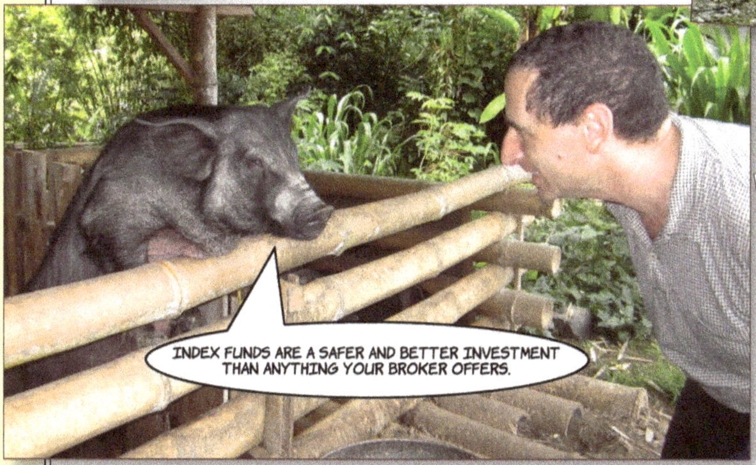
INDEX FUNDS ARE A SAFER AND BETTER INVESTMENT THAN ANYTHING YOUR BROKER OFFERS.

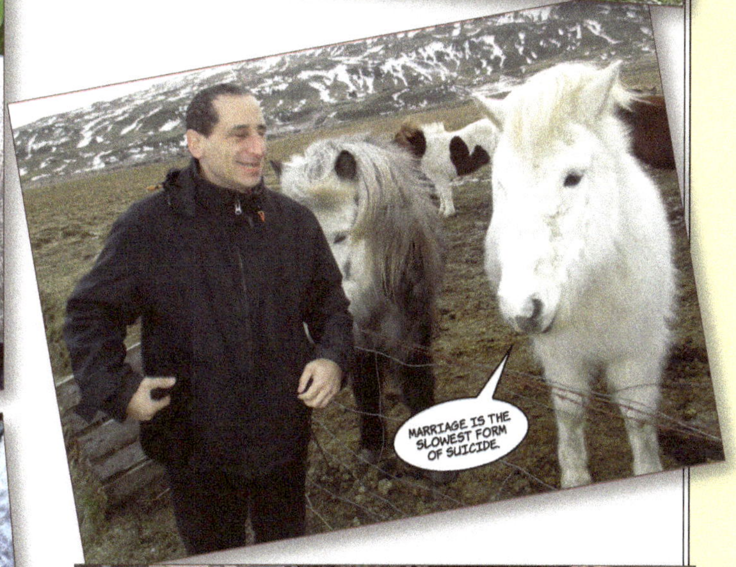
MARRIAGE IS THE SLOWEST FORM OF SUICIDE.

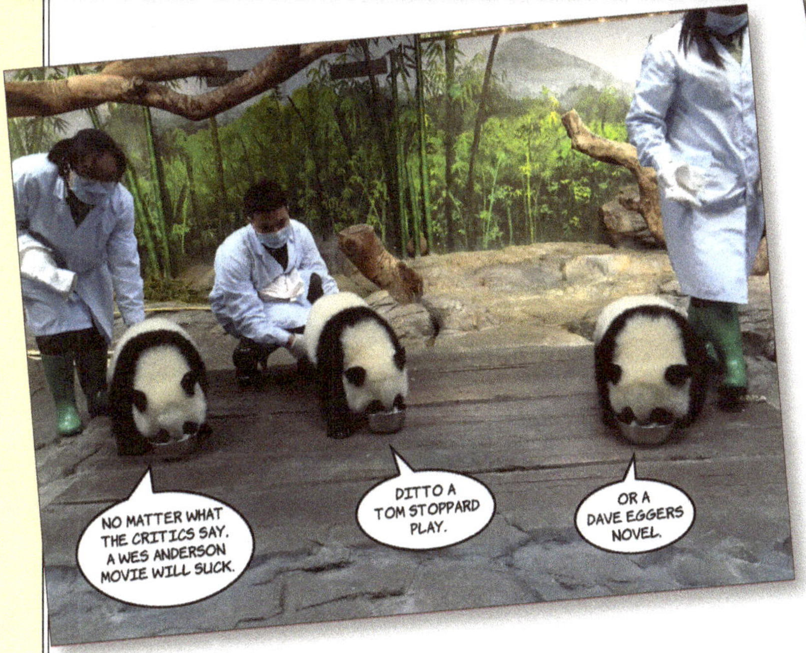
NO MATTER WHAT THE CRITICS SAY, A WES ANDERSON MOVIE WILL SUCK.
DITTO A TOM STOPPARD PLAY.
OR A DAVE EGGERS NOVEL.

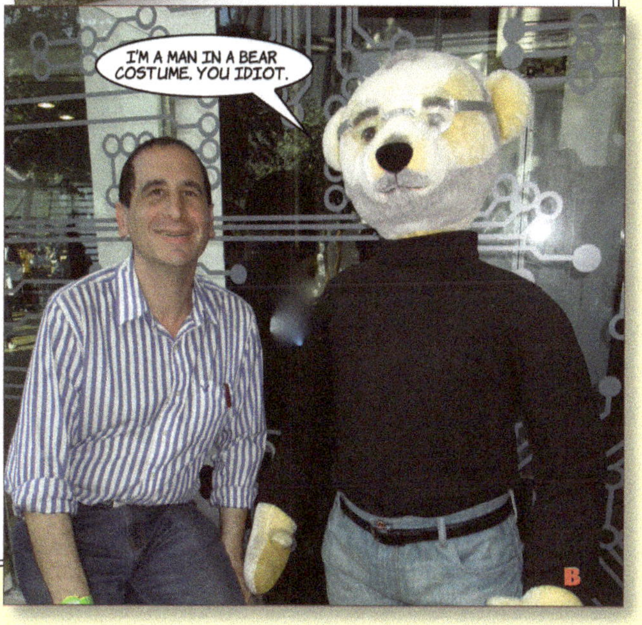
I'M A MAN IN A BEAR COSTUME, YOU IDIOT.

Photos by **DENISE REISS**

OWN ORIGINAL CARTOON ART

Become the owner—or gift giver—of original artwork.

Sam Gross

P.C. Vey 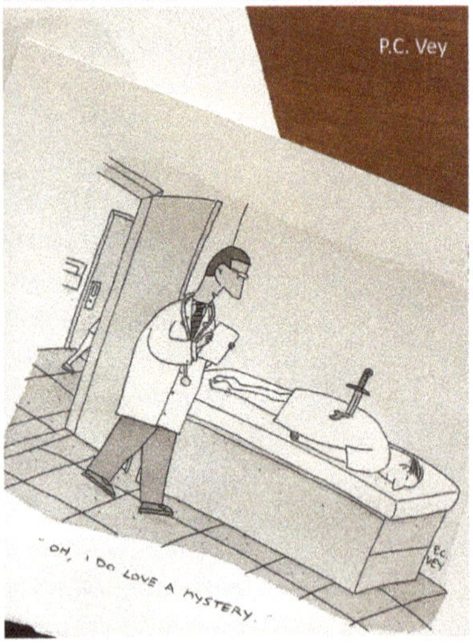 / George Booth

To enquire about your favorites please contact Samantha Vuignier:

SamanthaVuignier@CartoonCollections.com

or visit

CartoonCollections.com/originals

CARTOONCOLLECTIONS.COM

THE GOOD STUFF, continued from p 12

The Fabulous Furry Freak Bros. by Gilbert Shelton *(Shannon Wheeler)*
Familiar Faces by Mort Drucker *(Ian Baker)*
Forty Years with Mister Oswald by Russ Johnson *(Will Pfeifer)*
Ganges by Kevin Huizenga *(Alex Schmidt)*
The Golden Age by Kenneth Grahame, illustrated by Maxfield Parrish *(Sport Murphy)*
Good Grief, Charlie Brown! by Charles Schultz *(K.A. Polzin)*
Graphic Worlds of Peter Bruegel the Elder: Reproducing 63 Engravings and a Woodcut After Designs By Peter Bruegel the Elder *(David Chelsea)*
Graphis Annual (60s/70s) *(Sport Murphy)*
The Greatest of Marlys by Lynda Barry *(Andrew Weldon)*
Greetings from *This Modern World* by Tom Tomorrow *(K.A. Polzin)*
How to Eat Like a Child by Ephron & Koren *(Dylan Brody)*
The Huge Book of Hell by Matt Groening *(Andrew Weldon)*
Hyperbole and a Half by Allie Brosh *(Melissa Balmain)*
I Am Blind and My Dog is Dead by Sam Gross *(Ken Krimstein) (Ron Hauge) (Andrew Weldon) (John Jonik)*
I Die At Midnight by Kyle Baker *(Larry Doyle)*
I Go Pogo by Walt Kelly *(Sean Kelly)*
I Paint What I See by Gahan Wilson *(Ron Hauge)*
The Onion Magazine: The Iconic Covers by The Onion *(Andrew Weldon)*
If I Ran the Circus by Dr. Seuss *(Ken Krimstein)*
In Love with Art: Françoise Mouly's Adventures in Comics with Art Spiegelman by Jeet Heer *(Patrick Kennedy)*
In Me Own Words: The Autobiography of Bigfoot, by Graham Roumieu *(Andrew Weldon)*
Indexed by Jessica Hagy *(Riane Konc)*
Jimmy Corrigan, The Smartest Kid on Earth by Chris Ware *(Andrew Weldon)*
Jumping Up And Down on the Roof Throwing Bags Of Water on People by Mark Jacobs *(Ken Krimstein)*
Kampung Boy by Lat *(Phil Witte)*
Kavalier and Clay by Michael Chabon *(Mort Gerberg)*
Kingdom Come by Mark Waid and Alex Ross *(Joe Oesterle)*
KRAZY KAT and The Art of George Herriman by Patrick McDonnell and Karen O'Connell *(Sam Henderson) (Ron Hauge) (Patrick Kennedy)*
The Labyrinth by Saul Steinberg *(Ken Krimstein)*
Life on the Moon By Robert Grossman *(D. Watson)*
Little Nemo in Slumberland by Windsor McCay *(Joe Oesterle)*
A Little Yes and a Big No: The Autobiography of George Grosz *(Lance Hansen)*
The MAD Art Of Will Elder by Will Elder *(Sport Murphy)*
MAD's Vastly Overrated Al Jaffee *(JA Weinstein)*
Man the Beast/Wild Wild Women by Virgil Partch *(Sam Henderson)*
The Man in the Ceiling by Jules Feiffer *(Larry Doyle)*
Maus by Art Spiegelman *(Nick Spooner) (Ron Hauge)*
Maus II by Art Spiegelman *(Nick Spooner)*
Mind Your Own Business by Michael Rosen, illustrated by Quentin Blake *(Ian Baker)*
Miracle Man by Alan Moore & Alan Davis *(Shannon Wheeler)*

(TO BE CONTINUED NEXT ISSUE... B)

A History of the Greatest Magazine of All Time.

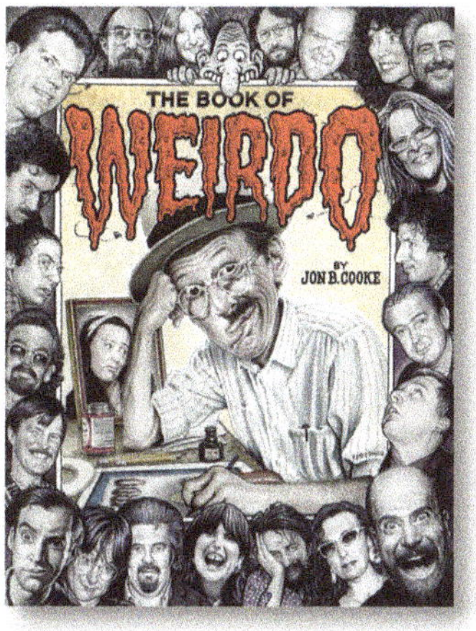

THE BOOK OF
WEIRDO
BY
JON B. COOKE

Well, that's what the folks over at the *Boing Boing* website called the new, 288-page hardcover, *The Book of Weirdo*. The feller said it was a "deep history," actually. We can attest it *is* insanely comprehensive…

In case you missed the '80s, *Weirdo* was R. Crumb's inspired answer to the "greed is good" Reagan era (and, if you come right down to it, artsy-fartsy comics, as well). Y'know, Robert Crumb: the guy who invented *ZAP Comix*, Fritz the Cat, Mr. Natural… and popularized the phrase, "Keep on Truckin.'" The wacked-out cartoonist who was the subject of Terry Zwigoff's 1994 film documentary… *that* R. Crumb.

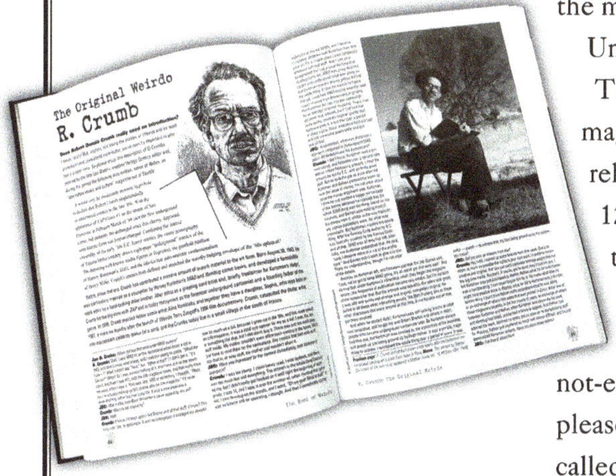

The Original Weirdo
R. Crumb

Anyway, Uncle Bob started and edited this humor comics anthology filled with savagely funny, sometimes puerile stuff. It was often politically incorrect to the Nth degree, and yet it was a haven for "outsider" artists, whether culled from the L.A. and New York City punk scenes, the mini-comics world, and street denizens of Berkeley, plus it welcomed into its pages the stories of a generation of women cartoonists.

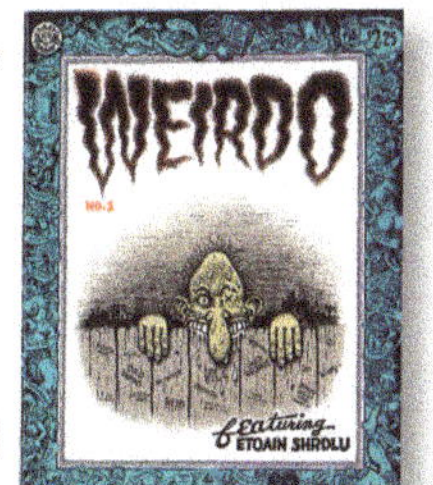

WEIRDO
featuring
ETOAIN SHRDLU

Weirdo lasted for 28 issues, a span when it was used as evidence in a landmark obscenity case, and it was edited by two other zany cartoonists, Peter Bagge and Aline Kominsky-Crumb. Upon its passing, the mag left behind a lingering impression among fellow comix artists. But, outside that crowd, the memory of *Weirdo* started to fade.

Until now.

This May, Last Gasp, the mag's original publisher, has released *The Book of Weirdo*, a 12-years-in-the-making retrospective which the not-easy-to-please Crumb called, "a great book… the definitive work on the subject." With a cover by master caricaturist Drew Friedman (who also provided the introduction), the tome includes recollections and testimonials of over 130 *Weirdo* contributors, plus an informed history of not only the mag, but the entire '80s alt comix scene. In fact, Crumb says, it's a "monumental statement on American culture and life in that dismal decade of Reagan, AIDS, widespread cocaine abuse, and the rise of the Yuppies…."

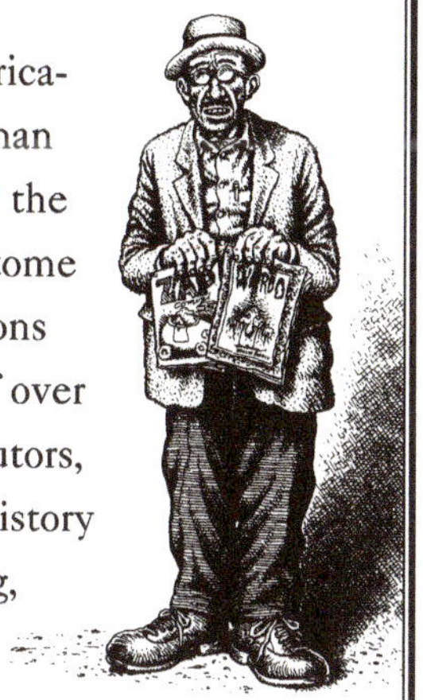

The opus also features comix by some talented modern-day weirdos too young to have appeared in the mag, and essays by the likes of Ivan Brunetti and others.

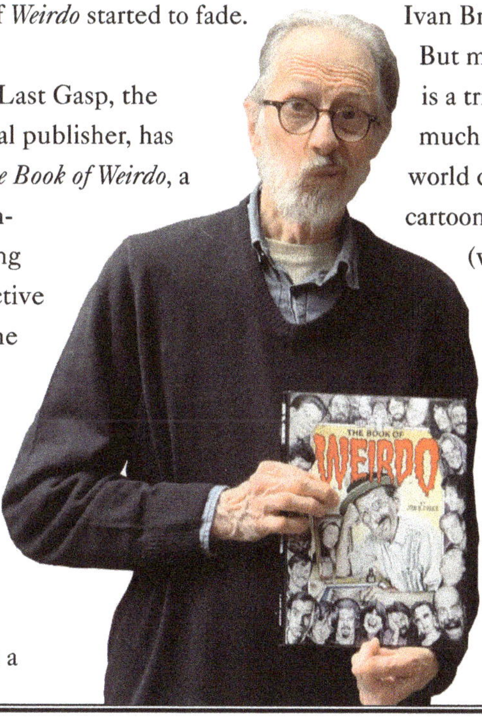

THE BOOK OF
WEIRDO

But most of all, the book is a tribute to the man much of the comix world calls the greatest cartoonist of all time (who had much of his finest work published in the pages of *Weirdo*).

So get the book, available at better bookstores and comic shops or via the publisher at *lastgasp.com*.

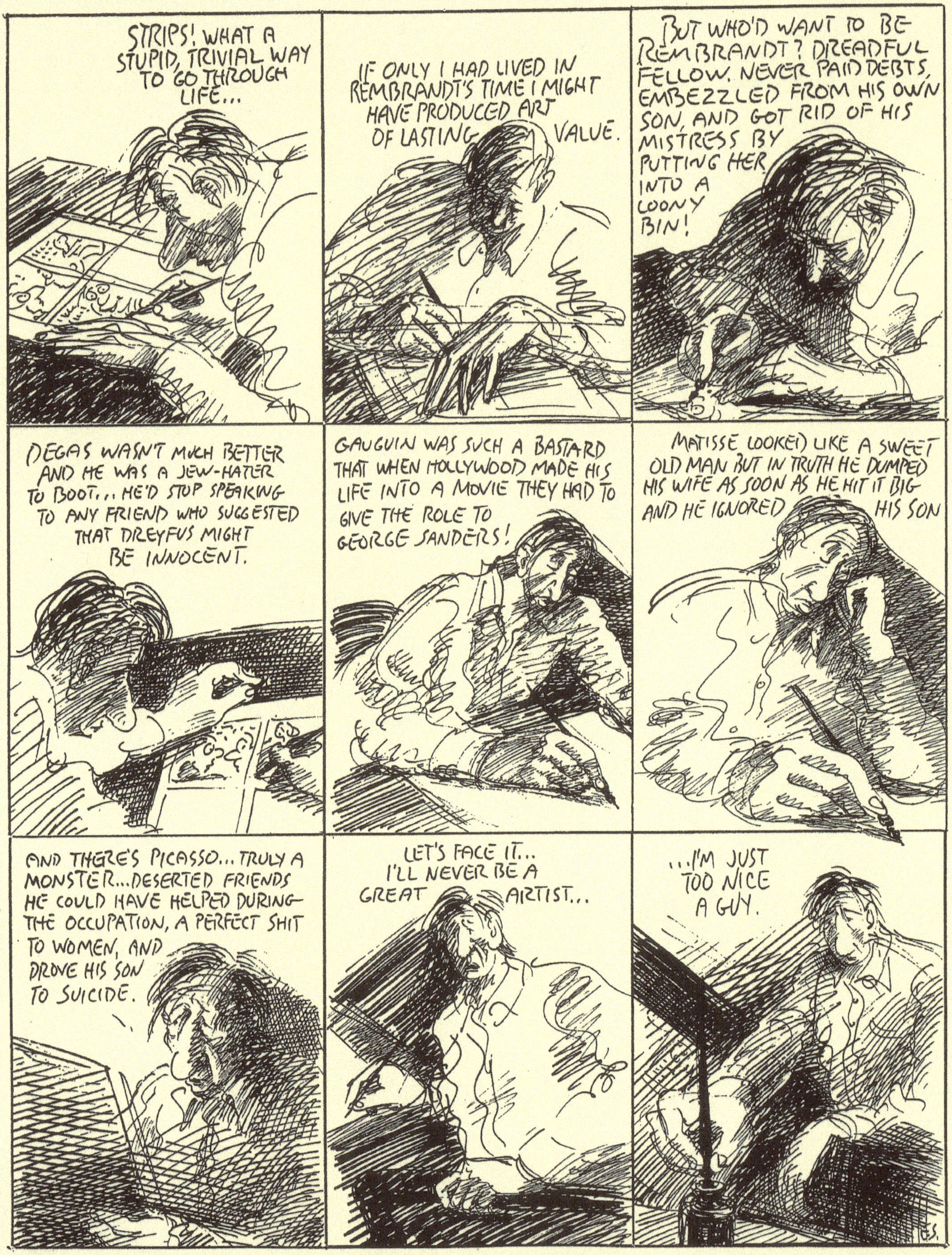
STRIPS! WHAT A STUPID, TRIVIAL WAY TO GO THROUGH LIFE...
IF ONLY I HAD LIVED IN REMBRANDT'S TIME I MIGHT HAVE PRODUCED ART OF LASTING VALUE.
BUT WHO'D WANT TO BE REMBRANDT? DREADFUL FELLOW. NEVER PAID DEBTS, EMBEZZLED FROM HIS OWN SON, AND GOT RID OF HIS MISTRESS BY PUTTING HER INTO A LOONY BIN!
DEGAS WASN'T MUCH BETTER AND HE WAS A JEW-HATER TO BOOT... HE'D STOP SPEAKING TO ANY FRIEND WHO SUGGESTED THAT DREYFUS MIGHT BE INNOCENT.
GAUGUIN WAS SUCH A BASTARD THAT WHEN HOLLYWOOD MADE HIS LIFE INTO A MOVIE THEY HAD TO GIVE THE ROLE TO GEORGE SANDERS!
MATISSE LOOKED LIKE A SWEET OLD MAN BUT IN TRUTH HE DUMPED HIS WIFE AS SOON AS HE HIT IT BIG AND HE IGNORED HIS SON
AND THERE'S PICASSO... TRULY A MONSTER...DESERTED FRIENDS HE COULD HAVE HELPED DURING THE OCCUPATION, A PERFECT SHIT TO WOMEN, AND DROVE HIS SON TO SUICIDE.
LET'S FACE IT... I'LL NEVER BE A GREAT ARTIST...
...I'M JUST TOO NICE A GUY.
E.S.

ED SOREL *(edwardsorel@gmail.com) is the author and illustrator of* **Mary Astor's Purple Diary** *(2016). A collection of his drawings,* **Profusely Illustrated**, *is scheduled for 2020.*

www.ingramcontent.com/pod-product-compliance
Lightning Source LLC
Chambersburg PA
CBHW061755290426
44108CB00029B/2998